Careers in Focus

Mechanics

SECOND EDITION

Ferguson
An imprint of ✔®Facts On File

Careers in Focus: Mechanics, Second Edition

Copyright © 2003 by Facts On File, Inc.

Ferguson
An imprint of Facts On File, Inc.
132 West 31st Street
New York NY 10001

Library of Congress Cataloging-in-Publication Data

Careers in focus. Mechanics. — 2nd ed.
    p. cm.
  ISBN 0-89434-477-3
  1. Machinery — Maintenance and repair — Vocational guidance.
  2. Mechanics (Persons) — Vocational guidance. I. Facts On File, Inc.
  II. Title: Mechanics.

TJ157.C37 2002
621.8'16'023--dc21   2002152744

Ferguson books are available at special discounts when purchased in bulk quantities for businesses, associations, institutions, or sales promotions. Please call our Special Sales Department in New York at (212) 967-8800 or (800) 322-8755.

You can find Ferguson Publishing on the World Wide Web at http://www.fergpubco.com

Managing Editor-Career Publications: Andrew Morkes
Senior Editor: Carol Yehling
Editor: Nora Walsh
Editorial Assistant: Laura Walsh

Cover photo courtesy U.S. Department of Agriculture

Printed in the United States of America

MP 10 9 8 7 6 5 4 3 2 1

This book is printed on acid-free paper.

Table of Contents

Introduction

Mechanics maintain and repair machines and mechanical systems. It would be difficult to name an area of your life that is not affected by the work of mechanics. From the moment that we get out of bed, mechanics of all types help us accomplish our daily tasks. *Automobile Service Technicians* keep your car running smoothly so that you can get to school or work. *Aircraft Mechanics* and *Diesel Mechanics* keep you safe when you travel by plane or train to far-away places. *General Maintenance Mechanics* keep your school, house, or workplace cool in the summer and warm in the winter. Did you ride an elevator today? If so, you can thank *Elevator Installers and Repairers* for your safe and quick trip. Been to the doctor lately? We bet that you never stopped to think about the *Biomedical Equipment Technicians* who maintain and repair the medical equipment used to diagnose and treat you. And what about the food you eat every day? *Agricultural Equipment Technicians* and *Farm Equipment Mechanics* maintain the equipment farmers use to plant and harvest the crops that eventually end up on your dinner table. There are even mechanics who repair the phones and computers you use to communicate (*Communications Equipment Technicians*); fix the musical instrument you might play (*Musical Instrument Repairers and Tuners*) in band or just for fun; or fix the mountain bike you ride after school or work (*Bicycle Mechanics*). In short, through mechanics, our lives have been thoroughly changed for the better.

The work of mechanics has been revolutionized by technological development. Workers in the industry are now often trained in electrical operations and computer programming to work on the more high-tech engines, parts, and systems that comprise products such as automobiles, appliances, and aircraft.

Each of the careers in this industry offers its own opportunities for advancement. Workers with the best potential, however, are those who become skilled at what they do, seek further training or education, and are always aware that changing technology and a global economy will affect jobs and opportunities in their industry. Trade associations and unions, in an effort to improve the skill level of workers and keep them in the industry, often offer different levels of training and certification. Some are short-term programs, but many last several years because of the knowledge required in specific jobs.

In order to advance in their careers, some mechanics choose to travel the road from apprentice to journey worker. Others choose to move from programming to designing, while still others become trainers and supervisors or move into technical sales and customer support. Those who dream of owning their own business should remember that most of the small businesses in this industry are owned by people who came up through the ranks.

Employment for mechanics is closely tied to the economic conditions within their specific industry. Although economic conditions did improve during the late 1990s, employment opportunities did not increase proportionately. Many companies laid off mechanics during the past decade and are hiring fewer workers than in the past. In addition, automation is affecting employment opportunities for many workers. The manufacturing industry has been revolutionized by highly productive, computer-controlled machining and turning centers that change their own tools; transfer machines that completely machine, assemble, and test mass-produced products; and innovative metal removal and forming systems. Robots and robotic equipment are becoming more common and are being used in many areas where the work is tedious, repetitious, or dangerous. Automated inspection equipment, such as electronic sensors, cameras, X rays, and lasers, is increasingly being used to test and inspect parts during production.

All these factors have affected the career outlook for mechanics. However, there will always be opportunities for mechanics who have advanced training and knowledge of the latest electronic and computer technology.

Each article in this book discusses a particular mechanics occupation in detail. The articles in *Careers in Focus: Mechanics* appear in Ferguson's *Encyclopedia of Careers and Vocational Guidance*, but they have been updated and revised with the latest information from the U.S. Department of Labor, professional organizations, and other sources. The **Overview** section is a brief introductory description of the duties and responsibilities of someone in this career. Oftentimes, a career may have a variety of job titles. When this is the case, alternative career titles are presented in this section. The **History** section describes the history of the particular job as it relates to the overall development of its industry or field. **The Job** describes the primary and secondary duties of the job. **Requirements** discusses high school and postsecondary education and training requirements, any certification or licensing necessary, and any other personal requirements for success in the job. **Exploring** offers suggestions on how to gain some experience in or knowledge of the particular job before making a firm educational and financial commitment. The focus is on what can be done while still in high school (or in the early years of college) to gain a better understanding of the job. The **Employers** section gives an overview of typical places of employment for the job. **Starting Out** discusses the best ways to land that first job, be it through the college placement office, newspaper ads, or personal contact. The **Advancement** section describes what kind of career path to expect from the job and how to get there. **Earnings** lists salary ranges and describes the typical fringe benefits. The **Work Environment** section describes the typical surroundings and conditions of employment—whether indoors or outdoors, noisy or quiet, social or independent, and so on. Also discussed are typical hours worked, any seasonal fluctuations, and the stresses and strains of the job. The **Outlook** section summarizes the job in terms of the general economy and industry projections. For the most part, Outlook information is obtained from the Bureau of Labor Statistics and is supplemented by information taken from professional associations. Job growth terms follow those used in the *Occupational Outlook Handbook:* Growth described as "much faster than the average" means an increase of 36 percent or more. Growth described as "faster than the average" means an increase of 21 to 35 percent. Growth described as "about as fast as the average" means an increase of 10 to 20 percent. Growth described as "little change or more slowly than the average" means an increase of 0 to 9 percent. "Decline" means a decrease of 1 percent or more.

Each article ends with **For More Information,** which lists organizations that can provide career information on training, education, internships, scholarships, and job placement.

Aeronautical and Aerospace Technicians

Overview

Aeronautical and aerospace technicians design, construct, test, operate, and maintain the basic structures of aircraft and spacecraft as well as propulsion and control systems. They work with scientists and engineers. Many aeronautical and aerospace technicians assist engineers in preparing equipment drawings, diagrams, blueprints, and scale models. They collect information, make computations, and perform laboratory tests. Their work may include working on various projects involving aerodynamics, structural design, flight-test evaluation, or propulsion problems. Other technicians estimate the cost of materials and labor required to manufacture the product, serve as manufacturers' field service technicians, and write technical materials.

History

Both aeronautical engineering and the aerospace industry had their births in the early 20th century. The very earliest machine-powered and heavier-than-air aircraft, such as the first one flown by Wilbur and Orville Wright in 1903, were crudely constructed and often the result of costly and dangerous trial-and-error experimentation.

As government and industry took an interest in the possible applications of this new invention, however, our knowledge of aircraft and the entire industry became more sophisticated. By 1908, for instance, the Wright brothers had received their first government military contract, and by 1909, the industry had expanded to include additional airplane producers, such as Glenn Curtiss in the United States and several others in France.

Aeronautical engineering and the aerospace industry have been radically transformed since those early days, mostly because of the demands of two world wars and the tremendous increases in scientific knowledge that have taken place during this century. Aviation and aerospace developments continued after the end of World War II. The factories and workers that built planes to support the war were in place and the industry took off, with the jet engine, rocket propulsion, supersonic flight, and manned voyages outside the earth's atmosphere among the major developments. As the industry evolved, aeronautical and aerospace engineers found themselves taking on increasingly larger projects and were more in need of trained and knowledgeable assistants to help them. Throughout the years, these assistants have been known as engineering aides, as engineering associates, and, most recently, as aerospace technicians and technologists. Their main task today is to take on assignments that require technical skills but do not necessarily require the scientist's or engineer's special training and education.

The Job

There are no clear-cut definitions of "aeronautical technology" and "aerospace technology"; in fact, many employers use the terms interchangeably. This lack of a clear distinction also occurs in education, where many schools and institutes offer similar courses under a variety of titles: aeronautical, aviation, or aerospace technology. In general, however, the term "aerospace industry" refers to manufacturers of all kinds of flying vehicles: from piston- and jet-powered aircraft that fly inside the earth's atmosphere, to rockets, missiles, satellites, probes, and all kinds of manned and unmanned spacecraft that operate outside the earth's atmosphere. The term "aeronautics" is often used within the aerospace industry to refer specifically to mechanical flight inside the earth's atmosphere, especially to the design and manufacture of commercial passenger and freight aircraft, private planes, and helicopters.

The difference between technicians and technologists generally refers to their level of education. Technicians generally hold associate's degrees, while technologists hold bachelor's degrees in aeronautical technology.

Whether they work for a private company working on commercial aircraft or for the federal government, aerospace technicians work side by side with engineers and scientists in all major phases of the design, production, and operation of aircraft and spacecraft technology. The aerospace technician position includes collecting and recording data; operating test equipment such as wind tunnels and flight simulators; devising tests to ensure quality control; modifying mathematical procedures to fit specific problems; laying out experimental circuits to test scientific theories; and evaluating experimental data for practical applications.

The following paragraphs describe jobs held by aerospace technicians; some may be used in other industries as well. Fuller descriptions of the work of some of these titles are provided in separate entries.

Aerospace physiological technicians operate devices used to train pilots and astronauts. These devices include pressure suits, pressure chambers, and ejection seats that simulate flying conditions. These technicians also operate other kinds of flight training equipment such as tow reels, radio equipment, and meteorological devices. They interview trainees about their medical histories, which helps detect evidence of conditions that would disqualify pilots or astronauts from further training.

Aircraft launch and recovery technicians work on aircraft carriers to operate, adjust, and repair launching and recovery equipment such as catapults, barricades, and arresting nets. They disassemble the launch and recovery equipment, replace defective parts, and keep track of all maintenance activities.

Avionics technicians repair, test, install, and maintain radar and radio equipment aboard aircraft and spacecraft.

Computer technicians assist mathematicians and subject specialists in checking and refining computations and systems, such as those required for predicting and determining orbits of spacecraft.

Drafting and design technicians convert the aeronautical engineer's specifications and rough sketches of aeronautical and aerospace equipment, such as electrical and mechanical devices, into accurate drawings that are used by skilled craft workers to make parts for aircraft and spacecraft.

Electronics technicians assist engineers in the design, development, and modification of electronic and electromechanical systems. They assist in the calibration and operation of radar and photographic equipment and also operate, install, troubleshoot, and repair electronic testing equipment.

Engineering technicians assist with review and analysis of post-flight data, structural failure, and other factors that cause failure in flight vehicles.

Industrial engineering technicians assist engineers in preparing layouts of machinery and equipment, work-flow plans, time-and-motion studies, and statistical studies and analyses of production costs to produce the most efficient use of personnel, materials, and machines.

Instrumentation technicians test, install, and maintain electronic, hydraulic, pneumatic, and optical instruments. These are used in aircraft systems and components in manufacturing as well as research and development. One important responsibility is to maintain their assigned research instruments. As a part of this maintenance, they test the instruments, take readings and calibration curves, and calculate correction factors for the instruments.

Liaison technicians check on the production of aircraft and spacecraft as they are being built for conformance to specifications, keeping engineers informed as the manufacturing progresses, and they investigate any engineering production problems that arise.

Mathematical technicians assist mathematicians, engineers, and scientists by performing computations involving the use of advanced mathematics.

Mechanical technicians use metalworking machines to assist in the manufacture of one-of-a-kind parts. They also assist in rocket-fin alignment, payload mating, weight and center-of-gravity measurements, and launch-tower erection.

Target aircraft technicians repair and maintain pilotless target aircraft. They assemble, repair, or replace aircraft parts such as cowlings, wings, and propeller assemblies and test aircraft engine operation.

Requirements

HIGH SCHOOL
A strong science and mathematics background is essential for entry into this field. High school courses that will be useful in preparing a student

for college-level study include algebra, trigonometry, physics, and chemistry. In addition to math and science, courses in social studies, economics, history, blueprint reading, drafting, and industrial and machine shop practice will provide a valuable background for a career in aerospace technology. Computer experience is also important. English, speech, and courses in the preparation of test reports and technical writing are extremely helpful to develop communication ability.

POSTSECONDARY TRAINING

There are a variety of training possibilities for potential aerospace technicians: two-, three-, or four-year programs at colleges or universities, junior or community colleges, technical institutes, vocational-technical schools, industry on-the-job training, or work-study programs in the military. Graduates from a two- or three-year program usually earn an associate's degree in engineering or science. Graduates from a four-year program earn a bachelor's degree in engineering or science; in addition, several colleges offer four-year degree programs in aeronautical technology. There are also many technical training schools, particularly in areas where the aerospace industry is most active, that offer training in aeronautical technology. However, many employers require graduates of such programs to complete a period of on-the-job training before they are granted full technician status. When selecting a school to attend, check the listings of such agencies as the Accreditation Board for Engineering and Technology and the regional accrediting associations for engineering colleges. Most employers prefer graduates of an accredited school.

In general, post-high school programs strengthen the student's background in science and mathematics, including pretechnical training. Beyond that, an interdisciplinary curriculum is more helpful than one that specializes in a narrow field. Other courses, which are basic to the work of the aeronautical scientist and engineer, should be part of a balanced program. These include basic physics, nuclear theory, chemistry, mechanics, and computers, including data-processing equipment and procedures.

CERTIFICATION OR LICENSING

Only a few aerospace technician positions require licensing or certification; however, certificates issued by professional organizations do enhance the status of qualified engineering technicians. Certification is usually required of those working with nuclear-powered engines or testing radioactive sources, for those working on aircraft in some test programs, and in some safety-related positions. Technicians and technologists working in areas related to national defense, and especially those employed by government agencies, are usually required to carry security clearances.

OTHER REQUIREMENTS

Aeronautical and aerospace technicians must be able to learn basic engineering skills. They should enjoy and be proficient in mathematics and the physical sciences, able to visualize size, form, and function. The Aerospace Industries Association of America advises that today's aerospace production worker must be strong in the basics of manufacturing, have a knowledge of statistics, and have the ability to work with computers.

Exploring

Visiting an aerospace research or manufacturing facility is one of the best ways to learn more about this field. Because there are so many such facilities connected with the aerospace industry throughout the United States, there is sure to be one in nearly every area. The reference department of a local library can help students locate the nearest facility.

Finding part-time or summer employment at such a facility is, of course, one of the best ways to gain experience or learn more about the field. Such jobs aren't available for all students interested in the field, but you can still find part-time work that will give you practical experience, such as in a local machine shop or factory.

Students should not overlook the educational benefits of visiting local museums of science and technology or aircraft museums or displays. The National Air and Space Museum at the Smithsonian Institution in Washington, DC, is one of the most comprehensive museums dedicated to aerospace. Some Air Force bases or naval air stations also offer tours to groups of interested students. The tours may be arranged by teachers or career guidance counselors.

The Junior Engineering Technical Society (JETS) provides students a chance to explore career opportunities in engineering and technology, enter academic competitions, and design model structures. JETS administers a competition that allows students to use their technology skills. The Tests of Engineering, Aptitude, Mathematics, and Science is an open-book, open-discussion engineering problem competition. If your school doesn't have a JETS chapter, check with other schools in your area; sometimes smaller schools can form cooperatives to offer such programs.

Employers

Aeronautical and aerospace technicians and technologists are principally employed by government agencies, commercial airlines, educational institutions, and aerospace manufacturing companies. Most technicians employed by manufacturing companies engage in research, development, and design; the remainder work in production, sales, engineering, installation and maintenance, and other related fields. Those employed by government and educational institutions are normally assigned to do research and perform specific problem-solving tasks. Airlines employ technicians to supervise maintenance operations and the development of procedures for new equipment.

Starting Out

The best way for students to obtain an aeronautical or aerospace technician's job is through their college or university's job placement office. Many manufacturers maintain recruiting relationships with schools in their area. Jobs may also be obtained through state employment offices, newspaper advertisements, applications for government employment, and industry work-study programs offered by many aircraft companies.

Advancement

Aeronautical and aerospace technicians continue to learn on the job. As they gain experience in specialized areas, employers turn to them as experts who can solve problems, create new techniques, devise new designs, or develop practice from theory.

Most advancement involves taking on additional responsibilities. For example, with experience, a technician may take on supervisory responsibilities, overseeing several trainees, assistant technicians, or others. Such a technician may also be assigned independent responsibility, especially on some tasks usually assigned to an engineer. Technicians with a good working knowledge of the company's equipment who have good personalities may become company sales or technical representatives. Technicians seeking further advancement are advised to continue their education. With additional formal education, a technician may become an aeronautical or aerospace engineer.

Earnings

Aerospace technology is a broad field, so earnings vary depending on a technician's specialty, educational preparation, and work experience. Starting salaries for most aerospace technicians generally ranged from $20,000 to $23,000 per year in the early 2000s, according to the U.S. Department of Labor. In 2000, the average annual salary for aerospace technicians was $53,340. Beyond that, salaries varied depending on specialty. For aircraft mechanics, including engine specialists, the average salary was around $40,560 in 2000, with starting pay at about $25,000 and pay for more experienced mechanics at over $56,000. Avionics technicians earned salaries that ranged from $27,500 to $56,200 in 2000.

Benefits depend on employers but usually include paid vacations and holidays, sick pay, health insurance, and a retirement plan. Salary increases will likely be held to a minimum over the next few years as the industry struggles to achieve a new balance after years of cutbacks. Nearly all companies offer some form of tuition reimbursement for further education. Some offer cooperative programs with local schools, combining classroom training with practical paid experience.

Work Environment

The aerospace industry, with its strong emphasis on quality and safety, is a very safe place to work. Special procedures and equipment make otherwise hazardous jobs extremely safe. The range of work covered means that the technicians can work in small teams in specialized research laboratories or in test areas that are large and hospital-clean.

Aerospace technicians are at the launch pad, involved in fueling and checkout procedures, and back in the blockhouse sitting at an electronic console. They work in large test facilities or in specialized shops, designing and fabricating equipment. They travel to test sites or tracking stations to construct facilities or troubleshoot systems. Working conditions vary with the assignment, but the work climate is always challenging, and co-workers are well-trained, competent people.

Aeronautical technicians may perform inside activities involving confined detail work, they may work outside, or they may combine both situations. Aeronautical and aerospace technicians work in many situations: alone, in small teams, or in large groups. Commonly, technicians participate in team projects, which are coordinated efforts of scientists, engineers, and technicians working on specific assignments. They concentrate on the practical aspects of the project and must get along well with and interact cooperatively with the scientists responsible for the theoretical aspects of the project.

Aerospace technicians must be able to perform under deadline pressure, meet strict requirements and rigid specifications, and deal with potentially hazardous situations. They must be willing and flexible enough to acquire new knowledge and techniques to adjust to rapidly changing technology. In addition, technicians need persistence and tenacity, especially when engaged in experimental and research tasks. They must be responsible, reliable, and willing to accept greater responsibility.

Aerospace technology is never far from the public's attention, and aeronautical technicians have the additional satisfaction of knowing that they are viewed as being engaged in vital and fascinating work.

Outlook

The *Career Guide to Industries* predicts that the civil aircraft sector of the aerospace industry will see strong growth (19 percent) through 2010, while the military aircraft sector is expected to decline about 4 percent during that same time period. With growth predicted in many areas, and losses in others, the overall job growth for aerospace technicians should be about as fast as the average through 2010.

Cutbacks made over the last 20 years have created a shrinking pool of new qualified workers for some positions, including technicians and skilled production workers, according to the Aerospace Industries Association of America (AIA). Many manufacturers in the aerospace Industry have responded to the decline of the 1990s by broadening their production to include other areas of technology. The AIA predicts aerospace companies will be looking for qualified technicians in fields such as laser optics, mission operations, hazardous materials procedures, production planning, materials testing, computer-aided design, and robotic operations and programming.

For More Information

For a listing of accredited technology programs, check the Web site or contact:
ACCREDITATION BOARD FOR ENGINEERING AND TECHNOLOGY, INC.
111 Market Place, Suite 1050
Baltimore, MD 21202-4012
Web: http://www.abet.org

Contact the AIA for publications with information on aerospace technologies, careers, and space.
AEROSPACE INDUSTRIES ASSOCIATION OF AMERICA (AIA)
1250 Eye Street, NW, Suite 1200
Washington, DC 20005-3924
Tel: 202-371-8400
Web: http://www.aia-aerospace.org

For career information and information on student branches of this organization, contact:
AMERICAN INSTITUTE OF AERONAUTICS AND ASTRONAUTICS
1801 Alexander Bell Drive, Suite 500
Reston, VA 20191-4344
Tel: 800-639-2422
Web: http://www.aiaa.org

This organization is dedicated to improving students' skills in math and science. For award and other information, contact:
AVIATION/AEROSPACE EDUCATION FOUNDATION
PO Box 3015
Syracuse, NY 13220-3015
Tel: 315-233-4837
Web: http://www.aaef.org

For career and scholarship information, contact:
GENERAL AVIATION MANUFACTURERS ASSOCIATION
1400 K Street, NW, Suite 801
Washington, DC 20005
Tel: 202-393-1500
Web: http://www.generalaviation.org

JETS has career information and offers high school students the opportunity to "try on" engineering through a number of programs and competitions. For more information, contact:
JUNIOR ENGINEERING TECHNICAL SOCIETY, INC. (JETS)
1420 King Street, Suite 405
Alexandria, VA 22314-2794
Tel: 703-548-5387
Email: jets@nae.edu
Web: http://www.jets.org

SEDS is an international organization of high school and college students dedicated to promoting interest in space. The United States national headquarters are located at the Massachusetts Institute of Technology. Contact:
STUDENTS FOR THE EXPLORATION AND DEVELOPMENT OF SPACE (SEDS)
MIT Room W20-445
77 Massachusetts Avenue
Cambridge, MA 02139-4307
Email: mitseds-officers@mit
Web: http://www.mit.edu/~mitseds

For more information on career choices and schools, contact:
AEROSPACE INDUSTRIES ASSOCIATION OF CANADA
60 Queen Street, Suite 1200
Ottawa, ON KIP 5Y7 Canada
Tel: 613-232-4297
Email: info@aiac.ca
Web: http://www.aiac.ca

Agricultural Equipment Technicians

Quick Facts

School Subjects
Mathematics
Technical/shop

Personal Skills
Mechanical/manipulative
Technical/scientific

Work Environment
Indoors and outdoors
Primarily multiple locations

Minimum Education Level
Some postsecondary training

Salary Range
$16,952 to $31,191 to $37,918+

Certification or Licensing
None available

Outlook
Little change or more slowly than
the average

Overview

Agricultural equipment technicians work with modern farm machinery. They assemble, adjust, operate, maintain, modify, test, and even help design it. This machinery includes automatic animal feeding systems; milking machine systems; and tilling, planting, harvesting, irrigating, drying, and handling equipment. Agricultural equipment technicians work on farms or for agricultural machinery manufacturers or dealerships. They often supervise skilled mechanics and other workers who keep machines and systems operating at maximum efficiency. Approximately 41,000 agricultural equipment technicians are employed in the United States.

History

The history of farming equipment stretches back to prehistoric times, when the first agricultural workers developed the sickle. In the Middle Ages, the horse-drawn plow greatly increased farm production, and in the early 1700s, Jethro Tull designed and built the first mechanical seed planter, further increasing production. The

Industrial Revolution brought advances in the design and use of specialized machinery for strenuous and repetitive work. It had a great impact on the agricultural industry, beginning in 1831 with Cyrus McCormick's invention of the reaper.

In the first half of the 20th century, governmental experiment stations developed high-yielding, standardized varieties of farm crops. This, combined with the establishment of agricultural equipment-producing companies, caused a boom in the production of farm machinery. In the late 1930s, the abundance of inexpensive petroleum spurred the development of gasoline- and diesel-run farm machinery. During the early 1940s, the resulting explosion in complex and powerful farm machinery multiplied production and replaced most of the horses and mules used on farms in the United States.

Modern farming is heavily dependent on very complex and expensive machinery. Highly trained and skilled technicians and farm mechanics are therefore required to install, operate, maintain, and modify it, thereby ensuring the nation's farm productivity. Recent developments in agricultural mechanization and automation make the career of agricultural equipment technician both challenging and rewarding. Sophisticated machines are being used to plant, cultivate, harvest, and process food; to contour, drain, and renovate land; and to clear land and harvest forest products in the process. Qualified agricultural equipment technicians are needed not only to service and sell this equipment, but also to manage it on the farm.

Farming has increasingly become a highly competitive, big business. A successful farmer may have hundreds of thousands or even millions of dollars invested in land and machinery. For this investment to pay off, it is vital to keep the machinery in excellent operating condition. Prompt and reliable service from the farm equipment manufacturer and dealer is necessary for the success of both farmer and dealer. Interruptions or delays because of poor service are costly for everyone involved. To provide good service, manufacturers and dealers need technicians and specialists who possess agricultural and engineering knowledge in addition to technical skills.

The Job

Agricultural equipment technicians work in a wide variety of jobs both on and off the farm. In general, most agricultural equipment technicians find employment in one of three areas: equipment manufacturing, equipment sales and service, and on-farm equipment management.

Equipment manufacturing technicians are involved primarily with the design and testing of agricultural equipment such as farm machinery; irrigation, power, and electrification systems; soil and water conservation equipment; and agricultural harvesting and processing equipment. There are two kinds of technicians working in this field: agricultural engineering technicians and agricultural equipment test technicians.

Agricultural engineering technicians work under the supervision of design engineers. They prepare original layouts and complete detailed drawings of agricultural equipment. They also review plans, diagrams, and blueprints to ensure that new products comply with company standards and design specifications. In order to do this they must use their knowledge of biological, engineering, and design principles. They also must keep current on all the new equipment and materials being developed for the industry to make sure the machines run at their highest capacity.

Agricultural equipment test technicians test and evaluate the performance of agricultural machinery and equipment. In particular, they make sure the equipment conforms with operating requirements, such as horsepower, resistance to vibration, and strength and hardness of parts. They test equipment under actual field conditions on company-operated research farms and under more controlled conditions. They work with test equipment and recording instruments such as bend-fatigue machines, dynamometers, strength testers, hardness meters, analytical balances, and electronic recorders.

Test technicians are also trained in methods of recording the data gathered during these tests. They compute values such as horsepower and tensile strength using algebraic formulas and report their findings using graphs, tables, and sketches.

After the design and testing phases are complete, other agricultural equipment technicians work with engineers to perform any necessary adjustments in the equipment design. By performing these functions under the general supervision of the design engineer, technicians do the engineers' "detective work" so the engineers can devote more time to research and development.

Large agricultural machinery companies may employ agricultural equipment technicians to supervise production, assembly, and plant operations.

Most manufacturers market their products through regional sales organizations to individual dealers. Technicians may serve as *sales representatives* of regional sales offices, where they are assigned a number of dealers in a given territory and sell agricultural equipment directly to them. They may also conduct sales-training programs for the dealers to help them become more effective salespeople.

These technicians are also qualified to work in sales positions within dealerships, either as *equipment sales workers* or *parts clerks.* They are required to perform equipment demonstrations for customers. They also appraise the value of used equipment for trade-in allowances. Technicians in these positions may advance to sales or parts manager positions.

Some technicians involved in sales become *systems specialists,* who work for equipment dealerships, assisting farmers in the planning and installation of various kinds of mechanized systems, such as irrigation or materials-handling systems, grain bins, or drying systems.

In the service area, technicians may work as *field service representatives,* forming a liaison between the companies they represent and the dealers. They assist the dealers in product warranty work, diagnose service problems, and give seminars or workshops on new service information and techniques. These types of service technicians may begin their careers as specialists in certain kinds of repairs. *Hydraulic specialists,* for instance, maintain and repair the component parts of hydraulic systems in tractors and other agricultural machines. *Diesel specialists* rebuild, calibrate, and test diesel pumps, injectors, and other diesel engine components.

Many service technicians work as service managers or parts department managers. *Service managers* assign duties to the repair workers, diagnose machinery problems, estimate repair costs for customers, and manage the repair shop.

Parts department managers in equipment dealerships maintain inventories of all the parts that may be requested either by customers or by the service departments of the dealership. They deal directly with customers, parts suppliers, and dealership managers and must have good sales and purchasing skills. They also must be effective business managers.

Technicians working on the farm have various responsibilities, the most important of which is keeping machinery in top working condition during the growing season. During off-season periods they may overhaul or modify equipment or simply keep the machinery in good working order for the next season.

Some technicians find employment as *on-farm machinery managers*, usually working on large farms servicing or supervising the servicing of all automated equipment. They also monitor the field operation of all machines and keep complete records of costs, utilization, and repair procedures relating to the maintenance of each piece of mechanical equipment.

Requirements

HIGH SCHOOL

You should take as many mathematics, technical/shop, and mechanical drawing classes as you can. Take science classes, including courses in earth science, to gain some insight into agriculture, soil conservation, and the environment. Look into adult education programs available to high school students; in such a program, you may be able to enroll in pre-engineering courses.

POSTSECONDARY TRAINING

A high school diploma is necessary, and some college and specialized experience is also important. A four-year education, along with some continuing education courses, can be very helpful in pursuing work, particularly if you're seeking jobs with the government.

Postsecondary education for the agricultural equipment technician should include courses in general agriculture, agricultural power and equipment, practical engineering, hydraulics, agricultural-equipment business methods, electrical equipment, engineering, social science, economics, and sales techniques. On-the-job experience during the summer is invaluable and frequently is included as part of the regular curriculum in these programs. Students are placed on farms, functioning as technicians-in-training. They also may work in farm equipment dealerships, where their time is divided between the sales, parts, and service departments. Occupational experience, one of the most important phases of the postsecondary training program, gives students an opportunity to discover which field best suits them and which phase of the business they prefer. Upon completion of this program, most technical and community colleges award an associate's degree.

OTHER REQUIREMENTS

The work of the agricultural equipment technician is similar to that of an engineer. You must have a knowledge of physical science and engineering principles and enough mathematical background to work with these principles. You must have a working knowledge of farm crops, machinery, and all agriculture-related products. You should be detail oriented. You should also have people skills, as you'll be working closely with professionals, other technicians, and farmers.

Exploring

If you live in a farming community, you've probably already had some experience with farming equipment. Vocational agriculture education programs in high schools can be found in most rural settings, in many suburban settings, and even in some urban schools. The teaching staff and counselors in these schools can provide considerable information about this career.

Light industrial machinery is now used in almost every industry. It is always helpful to watch machinery being used and to talk with people who own, operate, and repair it.

Summer and part-time work on a farm, in an agricultural equipment manufacturing plant, or in an equipment sales and service business offers opportunities to work on or near agricultural and light industrial machinery. Such a job may provide you with a clearer idea about the various activities, challenges, rewards, and possible limitations of this career.

Employers

Depending on their area of specialization, agricultural equipment technicians work for engineers, manufacturers, scientists, sales and services companies, and farmers. They can also find work with government agencies, such as the U.S. Department of Agriculture.

Starting Out

It is still possible to enter this career by starting as an inexperienced worker in a machinery manufacturer's plant or on a farm and learning machine technician skills on the job. However, this approach is becoming increasingly difficult due to the complexity of modern machinery. Because of this, some formal classroom training is usually necessary, and many people find it difficult to complete even part-time study of the field's theory and science while also working a full-time job.

The demand for qualified agricultural equipment technicians currently exceeds the supply. Operators and managers of large, well-equipped farms and farm equipment companies in need of employees keep in touch with colleges offering agricultural equipment programs. Students who do well during their occupational experience period usually have an excellent chance of going to work for the same employer after graduation. Many colleges have an interview day on which personnel representatives of manufacturers, distributors, farm owners or managers, and dealers are invited to recruit students completing technician programs. In general, any student who does well in a training program can expect employment immediately upon graduation.

Advancement

Opportunities for advancement and self-employment are excellent for those with the initiative to keep abreast of continuing developments in the farm equipment field. Technicians often attend company schools in sales and service or take advanced evening courses in colleges.

Earnings

Agricultural technicians working for the government may be able to enter a position at GS-5 (government wage scale), which paid $22,737 in 2002. Those with more education and specialized experience may be able to enter at GS-8, which paid $31,191. The U.S. Department of Labor reports that median hourly earnings for agricultural equipment technicians were $12.38 in 2000. Hourly pay ranged from less than $8.15 to more than $18.23. Those working on farms often receive room and board as a supplement to their annual salary. The salary that technicians eventually receive depends—as do most salaries—on individual ability, initiative, and the supply of skilled technicians in the field of work or locality. There is opportunity to work overtime during planting and harvesting seasons.

In addition to their salaries, most technicians receive fringe benefits such as health and retirement packages, paid vacations, and other benefits similar to those received by engineering technicians. Technicians employed in sales are usually paid a commission in addition to their base salary.

Work Environment

Working conditions vary according to the type of field chosen. Technicians who are employed by large farming operations will work indoors or outdoors depending on the season and the tasks that need to be done. Planning machine overhauls and the directing of such work usually are done in enclosed spaces equipped for it. As implied by its name, field servicing and repairs are done in the field.

Some agricultural equipment sales representatives work in their own or nearby communities, while others must travel extensively.

Technicians in agricultural equipment research, development, and production usually work under typical factory conditions. Some work in an office or laboratory; others work in a manufacturing plant; or, in some cases, field testing and demonstration are performed where the machinery will be used.

For technicians who assemble, adjust, modify, or test equipment and for those who provide customer service, application studies, and maintenance services, the surroundings may be similar to large automobile service centers.

In all cases, safety precautions must be a constant concern. Appropriate clothing, an acute awareness of one's environment, and careful lifting or hoisting of heavy machinery must be standard. While safety practices have improved greatly over the years, certain risks do exist. Heavy lifting may cause injury, and burns and cuts are always possible. The surroundings may be noisy and grimy. Some work is performed in cramped or awkward physical positions. Gasoline fumes and odors from oil products are a constant factor. Most technicians ordinarily work a 40-hour week, but emergency repairs may require overtime.

Outlook

The *Occupational Outlook Handbook* reports that employment of agricultural equipment technicians is expected to grow more slowly than the average through 2010. However, agricultural equipment businesses now demand more expertise than ever before. A variety of complex specialized machines and mechanical devices are steadily being produced and modified to help farmers improve the quality and productivity of their labor. These machines require trained technicians to design, produce, test, sell, and service them. Trained workers also are needed to instruct the final owners in the proper repair, operation, and maintenance of the machines.

In addition, the agricultural industry is adopting advanced computer and electronic technology. Computer skills are becoming more and more useful in this field. Precision farming will also require specialized training as more agricultural equipment becomes hooked up to satellite systems.

As agriculture becomes more technical, the agricultural equipment technician will assume an increasingly vital role in helping farmers solve problems that interfere with efficient production. These opportunities exist not only in the United States, but also worldwide. As agricultural economies everywhere become mechanized, inventive technicians with training in modern business principles will find expanding employment opportunities abroad.

For More Information

To read equipment sales statistics, agricultural reports, and other news of interest to agricultural equipment technicians, visit the AEM Web site.

ASSOCIATION OF EQUIPMENT MANUFACTURERS (AEM)
10 South Riverside Plaza, Suite 1220
Chicago, IL 60606-3710
Tel: 866-AEM-0442
Email: info@aem.org
Web: http://www.aem.org

At the FEMA Web site, you can learn about the association's publications and read industry news.

FARM EQUIPMENT MANUFACTURERS ASSOCIATION (FEMA)
1000 Executive Parkway, Suite 100
St. Louis, MO 63141-6369
Tel: 314-878-2304
Email: info@farmequip.org
Web: http://www.farmequip.org

Aircraft Mechanics

Overview

Aircraft mechanics examine, service, repair, and overhaul aircraft and aircraft engines. They also repair, replace, and assemble parts of the airframe (the structural parts of the plane other than the power plant or engine). There are about 173,000 aircraft mechanics working in the United States.

History

On December 17, 1903, Wilbur and Orville Wright made history's first successful powered flight. The Wright brothers—who originally built and repaired bicycles—designed, built, and repaired their airplane, including the engine, making them the first airplane mechanics as well. In the early years of aviation, most airplane designers filled a similar scope of functions, although many had people to assist them. As the aviation industry grew, the various tasks required to design, build, operate, and repair aircraft became more specialized. However, because of the instability of early planes and the uncertainty of the weather and other conditions, it was often necessary for pilots to have a strong working knowledge of how to repair and maintain their aircraft. In later years, one important route to becoming a pilot was to start as an aircraft mechanic.

As aircraft became capable of flying faster, for longer distances, and at higher altitudes, and especially after aircraft began to carry passengers, the role of the aircraft mechanic became vital to the safety of the aircraft and the growth of the aviation industry.

New technologies have continually been introduced into the design of aircraft, and mechanics needed to be familiar with all the systems, from the airframe to the engine to the control systems. The complexity of airplane design increased to the point where the mechanics themselves began to specialize. Some mechanics had the skills to work on the entire aircraft. Others were able to work on the airframe, on the engines, or on the power plant. Some mechanics functioned as repairers, who completed minor repairs to the plane. Mechanics were assisted by technicians, who were often training to become fully qualified mechanics. With the introduction of electronics into aircraft, some mechanics specialized as avionics technicians.

The Air Commerce Act of 1926 imposed regulations on the commercial airlines and their fleets. The Federal Aviation Agency, later called the Federal Aviation Administration (FAA), also established training and licensing requirements for the mechanics servicing the airplanes. Mechanics were also an important part of the armed forces, especially as the world entered World War II, in which air power became a vital part of successful military operations.

The growth of the general aviation industry, which includes all flights operated outside of the airlines, provided still more demand for trained mechanics. The introduction of ultralight aircraft in the 1970s brought air flight back to its origins: these craft were often sold as kits that the purchasers had to build and repair themselves.

The Job

The work of aircraft mechanics employed by the commercial airlines may be classified into two categories, that of line maintenance mechanics and overhaul mechanics.

Line maintenance mechanics are all-around craft workers who make repairs on all parts of the plane. Working at the airport, they make emergency and other necessary repairs in the time between when aircraft land and when they take off again. They may be told by the pilot, flight engineer, or head mechanic what repairs need to be made, or they may thoroughly inspect the plane themselves for oil leaks, cuts or dents in the surface and tires, or any malfunction in the radio, radar, and light equipment. In addition, their duties include changing oil, cleaning spark plugs, and replenishing the hydraulic and oxygen systems. They work as fast as safety permits so the aircraft can be put back into service quickly.

Overhaul mechanics keep the aircraft in top operating condition by performing scheduled maintenance, making repairs, and conducting inspections required by the FAA. Scheduled maintenance programs are based on the number of hours flown, calendar days, or a combination of these factors. Overhaul mechanics work at the airline's main overhaul base on either or both of the two major parts of the aircraft: the airframe, which includes wings, fuselage, tail assembly, landing gear, control cables, propeller assembly, and fuel and oil tanks; or the power plant, which may be a radial (internal combustion), turbojet, turboprop, or rocket engine.

Airframe mechanics work on parts of the aircraft other than the engine, inspecting the various components of the airframe for worn or defective parts. They check the sheet-metal surfaces, measure the tension of control cables, and check for rust, distortion, and cracks in the fuselage and wings. They consult manufacturers' manuals and the airline's maintenance manual for specifications and to determine whether repair or replacement is needed to correct defects or malfunctions. They also use specialized computer software to assist them in determining the need, extent, and nature of repairs. Airframe mechanics repair, replace, and assemble parts using a variety of tools, including power shears, sheet-metal breakers, arc and acetylene welding equipment, rivet guns, and air or electric drills.

Aircraft powerplant mechanics inspect, service, repair, and overhaul the engine of the aircraft. Looking through specially designed openings while working from ladders or scaffolds, they examine an engine's external appearance for such problems as cracked cylinders, oil leaks, or cracks or breaks in the turbine blades. They also listen to the engine in operation to detect sounds indicating malfunctioning components, such as sticking or burned valves. The test equipment used to check the engine's operation includes ignition analyzers, compression checkers, distributor timers, and ammeters. If necessary, the mechanics remove the engine from the aircraft, using a hoist or a forklift truck, and they take the engine apart. They use sensitive instruments to measure parts for wear and use X-ray and magnetic inspection equipment to check for invisible cracks. Worn or damaged parts are replaced or repaired, then the mechanics reassemble and reinstall the engine.

Aircraft mechanics adjust and repair electrical wiring systems and aircraft accessories and instruments; inspect, service, and repair pneumatic and hydraulic systems; and handle various servicing tasks, such as flushing crankcases, cleaning screens, greasing moving parts, and checking brakes.

Mechanics may work on only one type of aircraft or on many different types, such as jets, propeller-driven planes, and helicopters. For greater efficiency, some specialize in one section, such as the electrical system, of a particular type of aircraft. Among the specialists, there are airplane electricians; pneumatic testers and pressure sealer-and-testers; aircraft body repairers and bonded structures repairers, such as burnishers and bumpers; and air-conditioning mechanics, aircraft rigging and controls mechanics, plumbing and hydraulics mechanics, and experimental-aircraft testing mechanics. *Avionics technicians* are mechanics who specialize in the aircraft's electronic systems.

Mechanics who work for businesses that own their own aircraft usually handle all necessary repair and maintenance work. The planes, however, generally are small, and the work is less complex than in repair shops.

In small, independent repair shops, mechanics must inspect and repair many different types of aircraft. The airplanes may include small commuter planes run by an aviation company, private company planes and jets, private individually owned aircraft, and planes used for flying instruction.

Requirements

HIGH SCHOOL
The first requirement for prospective aircraft mechanics is a high school diploma. Courses in mathematics, physics, chemistry, and mechanical drawing are particularly helpful because they teach the principles involved in the operation of an aircraft, and this knowledge is often necessary to making the repairs. Machine shop, auto mechanics, or electrical shop are important courses for gaining many skills needed by aircraft mechanics.

POSTSECONDARY TRAINING
At one time, mechanics were able to acquire their skills through on-the-job training. This is rare today. Now most mechanics learn the job either in the armed forces or in trade schools approved by the FAA. The trade schools provide training with the necessary tools and equipment in programs that range in length from two years to 30 months. In considering

applicants for certification, the FAA sometimes accepts successful completion of such schooling in place of work experience, but the schools do not guarantee an FAA certificate.

The experience acquired by aircraft mechanics in the armed forces sometimes satisfies the work requirements for FAA certification, and veterans may be able to pass the exam with a limited amount of additional study. But jobs in the military service are usually too specialized to satisfy the FAA requirement for broad work experience. In that case, veterans applying for FAA approval will have to complete a training program at a trade school. Schools occasionally give some credit for material learned in the service. However, on the plus side, airlines are especially eager to hire aircraft mechanics with both military experience and a trade school education.

CERTIFICATION OR LICENSING

FAA certification is necessary for certain types of aircraft mechanics and is usually required to advance beyond entry-level positions. Most mechanics who work on civilian aircraft have FAA authorization as airframe mechanics, power plant mechanics, or avionics repair specialists. Airframe mechanics are qualified to work on the fuselage, wings, landing gear, and other structural parts of the aircraft; power plant mechanics are qualified to work on the engine. Mechanics may qualify for both airframe and power plant licensing, allowing them to work on any part of the plane. Combination airframe and power plant mechanics with an inspector's certificate are permitted to certify inspection work done by other mechanics. Mechanics without certification must be supervised by certified mechanics.

FAA certification is granted only to aircraft mechanics with previous work experience: a minimum of 18 months for an airframe or power plant certificate and at least 30 months working with both engines and airframes for a combination certificate. To qualify for an inspector's certificate, mechanics must have held a combined airframe and power plant certificate for at least three years. In addition, all applicants for certification must pass written and oral tests and demonstrate their ability to do the work authorized by the certificate.

OTHER REQUIREMENTS

Aircraft mechanics must be able to work with precision and meet rigid standards. Their physical condition is also important. They need more than average strength for lifting heavy parts and tools, as well as agility for reaching and climbing. And they should not be afraid of heights, since they may work on top of the wings and fuselages of large jet planes.

In addition to education and certification, union membership may be a requirement for some jobs, particularly for mechanics employed by major airlines. The principal unions organizing aircraft mechanics are the International Association of Machinists and Aerospace Workers and the Transport Workers Union of America. In addition, some mechanics are represented by the International Brotherhood of Teamsters, Chauffeurs, Warehousemen and Helpers of America.

Exploring

Working with electronic kits, tinkering with automobile engines, and assembling model airplanes are good ways of gauging your ability to do the kind of work performed by aircraft mechanics. A guided tour of an airfield can give you a brief overall view of this industry. Even better would be a part-time or summer job with an airline in an area such as the baggage department. Small airports may also offer job opportunities for part-time, summer, or replacement workers. You may also earn a Student Pilot (SP) license at the age of 16 and may gain more insight into the basic workings of an airplane that way. Kits for building ultralight craft are also available and may provide even more insight into the importance of proper maintenance and repair.

Employers

Of the roughly 173,000 aircraft mechanics currently employed in the United States, about two-thirds work for airlines or airports, according to the U.S. Department of Labor. Each airline usually has one main overhaul base, where most of its mechanics are employed. These bases are found along the main airline routes or near large cities, including New York, Chicago, Los Angeles, Atlanta, San Francisco, and Miami.

About one out of eight aircraft mechanics works for the federal government. Many of these mechanics are civilians employed at military aviation installations, while others work for the FAA, mainly in its headquarters in Oklahoma City. About one out of 10 mechanics works for aircraft assembly firms. Most of the rest are general aviation mechanics employed by independent repair shops at airports around the country, by businesses that use their own planes for transporting employees or cargo, by certified supplemental airlines, or by crop-dusting and air-taxi firms.

Starting Out

High school graduates who wish to become aircraft mechanics may enter this field by enrolling in an FAA-approved trade school. (Note that there are schools offering this training that do not have FAA approval.) These schools generally have placement services available for their graduates.

Another method is to make direct application to the employment offices of companies providing air transportation and services or the local offices of the state employment service, although airlines prefer to employ people who have already completed training. Many airports are managed by private fixed-base operators, which also operate the airport's repair and maintenance facilities. The field may also be entered through enlistment in the armed forces.

Advancement

Promotions depend in part on the size of the organization for which an aircraft mechanic works. The first promotion after beginning employment is usually based on merit and comes in the form of a salary increase. To advance further, many companies require the mechanic to have a combined airframe and power plant certificate, or perhaps an aircraft inspector's certificate.

Advancement could take the following route: journeyworker mechanic, head mechanic or crew chief, inspector, head inspector, and shop supervisor. With additional training, a mechanic may advance to engineering, administrative, or executive positions. In larger airlines, mechanics may advance to become flight engineers, then co-pilots and pilots. With business training, some mechanics open their own repair shops.

Earnings

Although some aircraft mechanics, especially at the entry level and at small businesses, earn little more than the minimum wage, the median annual income for aircraft mechanics was about $40,560 in 2000, according to the U.S. Department of Labor. The middle 50 percent earned between $32,552 and $49,192. The bottom 10 percent earned less than $25,085. Experienced mechanics can earn more than $56,000 per year. Mechanics with airframe and power plant certification earn more than those without it. Avionics technicians averaged $41,300 per year in 2000. Overtime, night shift, and holiday pay differentials are usually available and can greatly increase a mechanic's annual earnings.

Most major airlines are covered by union agreements. Their mechanics generally earn more than those working for other employers. Contracts usually include health insurance and often life insurance and retirement plans as well. An attractive fringe benefit for airline mechanics and their immediate families is free or reduced fares on their own and many other airlines. Mechanics working for the federal government also benefit from the greater job security of civil service and government jobs.

Work Environment

Most aircraft mechanics work a five-day, 40-hour week. Their working hours, however, may be irregular and often include nights, weekends, and holidays, as airlines operate 24 hours a day, and extra work is required during holiday seasons.

When doing overhauling and major inspection work, aircraft mechanics generally work in hangars with adequate heat, ventilation, and lights. If the hangars are full, however, or if repairs must be made quickly, they may work outdoors, sometimes in unpleasant weather. Outdoor work is frequent for line maintenance mechanics, who work at airports, because they must make minor repairs and preflight checks at the terminal to save time. To maintain flight schedules, or to keep from inconveniencing customers in general aviation, the mechanics often have to work under time pressure.

The work is physically strenuous and demanding. Mechanics often have to lift or pull as much as 70 pounds of weight. They may stand, lie, or kneel in awkward positions, sometimes in precarious places such as on a scaffold or ladder.

Noise and vibration are common when testing engines. Regardless of the stresses and strains, aircraft mechanics are expected to work quickly and with great precision.

Although the power tools and test equipment are provided by the employer, mechanics may be expected to furnish their own hand tools.

Outlook

The outlook for aircraft mechanics should improve over the course of the next decade. Employment opportunities will open up due to fewer young workers entering the labor force, fewer entrants from the military, and more retirees leaving positions. But the job prospects will vary according to the type of employer. Less competition for jobs is likely to be found at smaller commuter and regional airlines, at FAA repair stations, and in general aviation. These employers pay lower wages, and fewer applicants compete for their positions; higher-paying airline positions, which also include travel benefits, are more in demand among qualified applicants. Mechanics who keep up with technological advancements in electronics, composite materials, and other areas will be in greatest demand.

Employment of aircraft mechanics is likely to increase about as fast as the average through 2010, according to the U.S. Department of Labor. The demand for air travel and the number of aircraft created are expected to increase due to population growth and rising incomes. However, employment growth will be affected by the use of automated systems that make the aircraft mechanic's job more efficient.

For More Information

For career books and information about high school student membership, national forums, and job fairs, contact:
AVIATION INFORMATION RESOURCES, INC.
3800 Camp Creek Parkway, Suite 18-100
Atlanta, GA 30331
Tel: 800 JET JOBS
Web: http://www.jet-jobs.com

PROFESSIONAL AVIATION MAINTENANCE ASSOCIATION
Ronald Reagan Washington National Airport
Washington, DC 20001
Tel: 703-417-8800
Email: hq@pama.org
Web: http://www.pama.org

Appliance Service Technicians

Quick Facts

School Subjects
  Mathematics
  Physics
  Technical/shop
Personal Skills
  Mechanical/manipulative
  Technical/scientific
Work Environment
  Primarily indoors
  Primarily multiple locations
Minimum Education Level
  High school diploma
Salary Range
  $17,300 to $28,860 to $45,750+
Certification or Licensing
  Required by certain states
Outlook
  Little change or more slowly than
  the average

Overview

Appliance service technicians install and service many kinds of electrical and gas appliances, such as washing machines, dryers, refrigerators, ranges, and vacuum cleaners. Some repairers specialize in one type of appliance, such as air conditioners, while others work with a variety of appliances, both large and small, that are used in homes and business establishments. There are approximately 43,000 appliance technicians employed in the United States.

History

Although some small home appliances, including irons and coffee makers, were patented before the 20th century began, only a few types were in general use before the end of World War I. Around that time, however, more efficient and inexpensive electric motors were developed, which made appliances more affordable to the general public. In addition, electric and gas utility companies began extending their services into all parts of the nation. As a result, many new labor-saving appliances began to appear on the market. Eventually, consumers began to rely increasingly on a wide variety of machines to make everyday tasks easier and more pleasant, both at home and at work. Soon many kinds of equipment, such as washing machines and kitchen ranges, were considered an essential part of middle-class life.

Since the end of World War II, there has been a tremendous growth in the use and production of home appliances. The increasing use of appliances has created the need for qualified people to install, repair, and service them. Today's service technicians need a different mix of knowledge and skills than was needed by the appliance repairers of years ago, however, because today's appliances often involve complex electronic parts. The use of electronic components is advantageous to consumers because the electronic appliances are more reliable. However, the fact that modern appliances need fewer repairs means that the demand for appliance technicians is no longer growing as fast as the use of new appliances.

The Job

Appliance technicians use a variety of methods and test equipment to figure out what repairs are needed. They inspect machines for frayed electrical cords, cracked hoses, and broken connections; listen for loud vibrations or grinding noises; sniff for fumes or overheated materials; look for fluid leaks; and watch and feel other moving parts to determine if they are jammed or too tight. They may find the cause of trouble by using special test equipment made for particular appliances or standard testing devices such as voltmeters and ammeters. They must be able to combine all their observations into a diagnosis of the problem before they can repair the appliance.

Technicians often need to disassemble the appliance and examine its inner components. To do this, they often use ordinary hand tools such as screwdrivers, wrenches, and pliers. They may need to follow instructions in service manuals and troubleshooting guides. To understand electrical circuitry, they may consult wiring diagrams or schematics.

After the problem has been determined, the technician must correct it. This may involve replacing or repairing defective parts, such as belts, switches, motors, circuit boards, or gears. The technician also cleans, lubricates, and adjusts the parts so that they function as well and as smoothly as possible.

Those who service gas appliances may replace pipes, valves, thermostats, and indicator devices. In installing gas appliances, they may need to measure, cut, and connect the pipes to gas feeder lines and to do simple carpentry work such as cutting holes in floors to allow pipes to pass through.

Technicians who make service calls to homes and businesses must often answer customers' questions and deal with their complaints. They may explain to customers how to use the appliance and advise them about proper care. These technicians are often responsible for ordering parts from catalogs and recording the time spent, the parts used, and whether a warranty applies to the repair job. They may need to estimate the cost of repairs, collect payment for their work, and sell new or used appliances. Many technicians who make service calls drive light trucks or automobiles equipped with two-way radios or cellular phones so that as soon as they finish one job, they can be dispatched to another.

Many appliance service technicians repair all different kinds of appliances; there are also those who specialize in one particular kind or one brand of appliance. *Window air-conditioning unit installers and technicians,* for example, work only with portable window units, while *domestic air-conditioning technicians* work with both window and central systems in homes.

Household appliance installers specialize in installing major household appliances, such as refrigerators, freezers, washing machines, clothes dryers, kitchen ranges, and ovens; *household appliance technicians* maintain and repair these units.

Small electrical appliance technicians repair portable household electrical appliances such as toasters, coffee makers, lamps, hair dryers, fans, food processors, dehumidifiers, and irons. Customers usually bring these types of appliances to service centers to have them repaired.

Gas appliance technicians install, repair, and clean gas appliances such as ranges or stoves, heaters, and gas furnaces. They also advise customers on the safe, efficient, and economical use of gas.

Requirements

HIGH SCHOOL
Appliance technicians usually must be high school graduates with some knowledge of electricity (especially wiring diagrams) and, if possible, electronics. If you are interested in this field, you should take as many shop classes as possible to gain a familiarity with machines and tools. Electrical shop is particularly helpful because of the increasing use of electronic components in appliances. Mathematics and physics are good choices to build a knowledge of mechanical principles.

POSTSECONDARY TRAINING

Prospective technicians are sometimes hired as helpers and acquire most of their skills through on-the-job experience. Some employers assign such helpers to accompany experienced technicians when they are sent to do repairs in customers' homes and businesses. The trainees observe and assist in diagnosing and correcting problems with appliances. Other employers assign helpers to work in the company's service center, where they learn how to rebuild used appliances and make simple repairs. At the end of six to 12 months, they usually know enough to make most repairs on their own, and they may be sent on unsupervised service calls.

An additional one to two years of experience is often required for trainees to become fully qualified. Trainees may attend service schools sponsored by appliance manufacturers and also study service manuals to familiarize themselves with appliances, particularly new models. Reading manuals and attending courses are a continuing part of any technician's job.

Many technicians train at public or private technical and vocational schools that provide formal classroom training and laboratory experience in the service and repair of appliances. The length of these programs varies, although most last between one and two years. Correspondence courses that teach basic appliance repair are also available. Although formal training in the skills needed for appliance repairing can be a great advantage for job applicants, newly graduated technicians should expect additional on-the-job training to acquaint them with the particular work done in their new employer's service center.

CERTIFICATION OR LICENSING

In some states, appliance technicians may need to be licensed or registered. Licenses are granted to applicants who meet certain standards of education, training, and experience and who pass an examination. Since 1994, the Environmental Protection Agency has required certification for all technicians who work with appliances containing refrigerants known as chlorofluorocarbons. Since these refrigerants can be harmful to the environment, technicians must be educated and tested on their handling in order to achieve certification to work with them.

The National Appliance Service Technician Certification Program (NASTeC) offers certification on four levels: refrigeration and air conditioning; cooking; laundry, dishwashing, and food disposers; and universal technician (all three specialties). To earn NASTeC certification, candidates must pass a Basic Skills Exam and at least one of the three specialty exams. Technicians who pass all four exams are certified as

NASTeC Universal Technicians. There are more than 400 test administrators who give the tests at locations such as local technician schools. Technicians should arrange for their test times.

The Professional Service Association (PSA) also offers certification to appliance repairers. The PSA offers the following certifications to technicians who pass an examination: Certified Appliance Professional, Master Certified Appliance Professional, Certified Service Manager, and Certified Consumer Specialist. Certification is valid for four years, at which time technicians must apply for recertification and pass another examination. Certified technicians who complete at least 15 credit hours of continuing education annually during the four years do not need to retake the examination to gain recertification.

OTHER REQUIREMENTS

Technicians must possess not only the skills and mechanical aptitude necessary to repair appliances but also skills in consumer relations. They must be able to deal courteously with all types of people and be able to convince their customers that the products they repair will continue to give satisfactory service for some time to come. Technicians must work effectively with little supervision, since they often spend their days alone, going from job to job. It is necessary that they be accurate and careful in their repair work, since their customers rely on them to correct problems properly.

Exploring

You can explore the field by talking to employees of local appliance service centers and dealerships. These employees may know about part-time or summer jobs that will enable you to observe and assist with repair work. You can also judge interest and aptitude for this work by taking shop courses, especially electrical shop, and assembling electronic equipment from kits

Employers

Currently, there are about 43,000 appliance technicians employed throughout the United States in service centers, appliance manufacturers, retail dealerships, and utility companies. They may also be self-employed in independent repair shops or work at companies that service specific types of appliances, such as coin-operated laundry equipment and dry-cleaning machines.

Starting Out

One way of entering this occupation is to become a helper in a service center where the employer provides on-the-job training to qualified workers. To find a helper's job, prospective technicians should apply directly to local service centers or appliance dealerships. They also can watch area newspaper classified ads for entry-level jobs in appliance service and repair.

For those who have graduated from a technical or vocational program, their schools' placement offices may also prove helpful.

Advancement

Advancement possibilities for appliance service technicians depend primarily on their place of employment. In a small service center of three to five people, advancement to a supervisory position will likely be slow because the owner usually performs most of the supervisory and administrative tasks. However, pay incentives do exist in smaller service centers that encourage technicians to assume a greater share of the management load. Technicians working for large retailers, factory service centers, or gas or electric utility companies may be able to progress to supervisor, assistant service manager, or service manager.

Another advancement route leads to teaching at a factory service training school. A technician who knows the factory's product, works with proficiency, and speaks effectively to groups can conduct classes to train other technicians. Technical and vocational schools that offer courses in appliance repair work may also hire experienced repairers to teach classes.

Some service technicians aspire to opening an independent repair business or service center. This step usually requires a knowledge of business management and marketing and a significant investment in tools, parts, vehicles, and other equipment.

Some technicians who work for appliance manufacturers move into positions where they write service manuals, sell appliances, or act as manufacturers' service representatives to independent service centers

Earnings

The earnings of appliance technicians vary widely according to geographic location, type of equipment serviced, workers' skills and experience, and other factors. In 2000, the U.S. Department of Labor reported that the median annual salary for home appliance technicians was about $28,860. At the low end of the salary scale, technicians earned approximately $17,300. Technicians at the high end of the pay scale earned $45,750 or more per year. Trainees are usually paid less than technicians who have completed their training period. Employees of gas utility companies and other large companies generally command higher hourly wages than those who work for service centers. Some service centers, however, offer incentives for technicians to increase their productivity. Some of these incentive plans are very lucrative and can allow a proficient worker to add considerably to his or her salary.

Opportunities for overtime pay are most favorable for repairers of major appliances, such as refrigerators, stoves, and washing machines. In addition to regular pay, many workers receive paid vacations and sick leave, health insurance, and other benefits such as employer contributions to retirement pension plans.

Work Environment

Appliance technicians generally work a standard 40-hour week, although some work evenings and weekends. Repairers who work on cooling equipment, such as refrigerators and air conditioners, may need to put in extra hours during hot weather. In general, there is little seasonal fluctuation of employment in this occupation, since repairs on appliances are needed at all times of the year and the work is done indoors.

Technicians encounter a variety of working conditions depending on the kinds of appliances they install or repair. Those who fix small appliances work indoors at a bench and seldom have to handle heavy objects. Their workplaces are generally well lighted, properly ventilated, and equipped with the necessary tools.

Repairers who work on major appliances must deal with a variety of situations. They normally do their work on-site, so they may spend several hours each day driving from one job to the next. To do repairs, they may have to work in small or dirty spaces or in other uncomfortable conditions. They may have to crawl, bend, stoop, crouch, or lie down to carry out some repairs, and they may have to move heavy items. Because they work in a variety of environments, they may encounter unpleasant situations, such as dirt, odors, or pest infestation.

In any appliance repair work, technicians must follow good safety procedures, especially when handling potentially dangerous tools, gas, and electric currents.

Outlook

The U.S. Department of Labor reports that through 2010 the total number of repairers is expected to increase more slowly than the average. Although Americans will certainly continue buying and using more appliances, today's machines are often made with electronic components that require fewer repairs than their nonelectronic counterparts. Thus, the dependability of the technology built into these new appliances will restrain growth in the repair field. Most openings that arise will be due to workers leaving their jobs who must be replaced.

For More Information

For information on certification, contact:
NATIONAL APPLIANCE SERVICE TECHNICIAN CERTIFICATION PROGRAM
10 East 22nd Street, Suite 310
Lombard, IL 60148
Web: http://www.nastecnet.org

For information on the Refrigerant Recovery Certification Test Program, contact:
NORTH AMERICAN RETAIL DEALERS ASSOCIATION
10 East 22nd Street, Suite 310
Lombard, IL 60148-6191
Web: http://www.narda.com

For information on careers and certification, contact:
PROFESSIONAL SERVICE ASSOCIATION
71 Columbia Street
Cohoes, NY 12047
Web: http://www.psaworld.com

Automobile Collision Repairers

Quick Facts

School Subjects
  Computer science
  Technical/shop
Personal Skills
  Following instructions
  Mechanical/manipulative
Work Environment
  Primarily indoors
  Primarily one location
Minimum Education Level
  Some postsecondary training
Salary Range
  $17,659 to $31,200 to $54,205+
Certification or Licensing
  Recommended
Outlook
  About as fast as the average

Overview

Automobile collision repairers repair, replace, and repaint damaged body parts of automobiles, buses, and light trucks. They use hand tools and power tools to straighten bent frames and body sections, replace badly damaged parts, smooth out minor dents and creases, remove rust, fill small holes or dents, and repaint surfaces damaged by accident or wear. Some repairers also give repair estimates. There are approximately 221,000 automobile collision repairers working in the United States.

History

The proliferation of the automobile in American society in the 1920s meant new opportunities for many who had not traveled far beyond their hometown. It also created something else by the thousands—jobs. One profession necessitated by America's new love for automobiles was that of the collision repairer. With ill-prepared roads suddenly overrun by inexperienced drivers, accidents and breakdowns became a common problem.

Automobiles were significantly simpler in the early years. Body repairs often could be performed by the owner or someone with general mechanical aptitude. Minor body dents, if they did not affect driving, were usually left alone. As cars became more complex and as people grew ever more fond of their automobiles, the need for qualified collision repairers grew. Automobiles suddenly became major status symbols, and people were no longer indifferent to minor dents and fender-benders. To many, dents were intolerable. New body styles and materials made body repairs a difficult job. To meet this new demand, some automobile mechanics shifted their focus from repairs under the hood to repairs to the body of automobiles.

By the 1950s, automobile body repair garages were common in cities throughout the United States. More drivers carried vehicle insurance to protect against loss due to an accident. The insurance industry began to work more closely with automobile collision repairers. Since traffic control methods and driving rules and regulations were not very well established, frequent car accidents kept these repair garages busy year-round. Most collision repairers learned the trade through hands-on experience as an apprentice or on their own through trial and error. When automakers began packing their cars with new technology, involving complex electrical circuitry, computer-controlled mechanisms, and new materials, as well as basic design changes, collision repairers found themselves in need of comprehensive training.

The Job

Automobile collision repairers repair the damage vehicles sustain in traffic accidents and through normal wear. Repairers straighten bent bodies, remove dents, and replace parts that are beyond repair. Just as a variety of skills are needed to build an automobile, so a range of skills is needed to repair body damage to vehicles. Some body repairers specialize in certain areas, such as painting, welding, glass replacement, or air bag replacement. All collision repairers should know how to perform common repairs, such as realigning vehicle frames, smoothing dents, and removing and replacing panels.

Vehicle bodies are made from a wide array of materials, including steel, aluminum, metal alloys, fiberglass, and plastic, with each material requiring a different repair technique. Most repairers can work with all these materials, but as car manufacturers produce vehicles with an increasing proportion of lightweight fiberglass, aluminum, and plastic parts, more repairers specialize in repairing these specific materials.

Collision repairers frequently must remove car seats, accessories, electrical components, hydraulic windows, dashboards, and trim to get to the parts that need repair. If the frame or a body section of the vehicle has been bent or twisted, frame repairers and straighteners can sometimes restore it to its original alignment and shape. This is done by chaining or clamping it to an alignment machine, which uses hydraulic pressure to pull the damaged metal into position. Repairers use specialty measuring equipment to set all components, such as engine parts, wheels, headlights, and body parts, at manufacturer's specifications.

After the frame is straightened, dents in the metal body can be corrected in several different ways, depending on how deep they are. If any part is too badly damaged to repair, the collision repairers remove it with hand tools, a pneumatic metal-cutting gun, or an acetylene torch, then they weld on a replacement. Some dents can be pushed out with hydraulic jacks, pneumatic hammers, prying bars, and other hand tools. To smooth small dents and creases, collision repairers may position small anvils, called dolly blocks, against one side of the dented metal. They then hit the opposite side of the metal with various specially designed hammers. Tiny pits and dimples are removed with pick hammers and punches. Dents that cannot be corrected with this treatment may be filled with solder or a puttylike material that becomes hard like metal after it cures. When the filler has hardened, the collision repairers file, grind, and sand the surface smooth in the correct contour and prepare it for painting. In many shops the final sanding and painting are done by other specialists, who may be called *automotive painters.*

Since more than the body is usually damaged in a major automobile accident, repairers have other components to repair. Advanced vehicle systems on new cars such as anti-lock brakes, air bags, and other "passive restraint systems" require special training to repair. Steering and suspension, electrical components, and glass are often damaged and require repair, removal, or replacement.

Automotive painting is a highly skilled, labor-intensive job that requires a fine eye and attention to detail for the result to match the pre-accident condition. Some paint jobs require that less than the whole vehicle be painted. In this case, the painter must mix pigments to match the original color. This can be difficult if the original paint is faded, but computer technology is making paint matching easier.

A major part of the automobile collision repairer's job is assessing the damage and providing an estimate on the cost to repair it. Sometimes, the damage to a vehicle may cost more to repair than the vehicle is worth. When this happens, the vehicle is said to be "totaled," a term used by collision repairers as well as insurance companies. Many body repair shops offer towing services and will coordinate the transfer of a vehicle from the accident scene as well as the transfer of a totaled vehicle to a scrap dealer who will salvage the useable parts.

The shop supervisor or repair service estimator prepares the estimate. They inspect the extent of the damage to determine if the vehicle can be repaired or must be replaced. They note the year, model, and make of the car to determine type and availability of parts. Based on past experience with similar types of repair and general industry guidelines, estimates are calculated for parts and labor and then submitted to the customer's insurance company. One "walk around" a car will tell the collision repairer what needs to be investigated. Since a collision often involves "hidden" damage, supervisors write up repair orders with specific instructions so no work is missed or, in some cases, done unnecessarily. Repair orders often indicate only specific parts are to be repaired or replaced. Collision repairers generally work on a project by themselves with minimal supervision. In large, busy shops, repairers may be assisted by helpers or apprentices.

Requirements

HIGH SCHOOL

Technology demands more from the collision repairer than it did 10 years ago. In addition to automotive and shop classes, high school students should take mathematics, English, and computer classes. Adjustments and repairs to many car components require numerous computations, for which good mathematics skills are essential. Reading comprehension skills will help a collision repairer understand complex repair manuals and trade journals that detail new technology. Oral communication skills are also important to help customers understand their options. In addition, computers are common in most collision repair shops. They keep track of customer histories and parts and often detail repair procedures. Use of computers in repair shops will only increase in the future, so students will benefit from a basic knowledge of them.

POSTSECONDARY TRAINING

A wide variety of training programs are offered at community colleges and vocational schools and by independent organizations and manufacturers. As automotive technology changes, the materials and methods involved in repair work change. With new high-strength steels, aluminum, and plastics becoming ever more common in newer vehicles and posing new challenges in vehicle repair, repairers will need special training to detect the many hidden problems that occur beyond the impact spot. Postsecondary training programs provide students with the necessary, up-to-date skills needed for repairing today's vehicles.

CERTIFICATION OR LICENSING
Entry-level technicians in the industry can demonstrate their qualifications through certification by the National Automotive Technicians Education Foundation (NATEF), an affiliate of the National Institute for Automotive Service Excellence (ASE). Certification is voluntary, but it assures students that the program they enroll in meets the standards employers expect from their entry-level employees. Many trade and vocational schools throughout the country have affiliation with the NATEF. To remain certified, repairers must take the examination again within five years. Another industry-recognized standard of training is provided by the Inter-Industry Conference on Auto Collision Repair (I-CAR). I-CAR provides training for students and experienced technicians alike in the areas of advanced vehicle systems, aluminum repair and welding, complete collision repair, electronics for collision repair, finish matching, and other specialty fields.

OTHER REQUIREMENTS
Automobile collision repairers are responsible for providing their own hand tools at an investment of approximately $6,000 to $20,000 or more, depending on the technician's specialty. It is the employer's responsibility to provide the larger power tools and other test equipment. Skill in handling both hand and power tools is essential for any repairer. Since each collision repair job is unique and presents a different challenge, repairers often must be resourceful in their method of repair.

While union membership is not a requirement for collision repairers, many belong to the International Association of Machinists and Aerospace Workers; the International Union, United Automobile, Aerospace and Agricultural Implement Workers of America; the Sheet Metal Workers International Association; or the International Brotherhood of Teamsters, Chauffeurs, Warehousemen and Helpers of America. Most collision repairers who are union members work for large automobile dealers, trucking companies, and bus lines.

Exploring

Many community colleges and park districts offer general auto maintenance, mechanics, and body repair workshops where students can get additional practice working on cars and learn from experienced instructors. Trade magazines such as *Automotive Body Repair News* (http://www.abrn.com) are an excellent source for learning what's new in the industry. Such publications may be available at larger public libraries or vocational schools. Many journals also post current and archived articles on the Internet.

Working on cars as a hobby provides invaluable firsthand experience in repair work. A part-time job in a repair shop or dealership allows a feel for the general atmosphere and the kinds of problems repairers face on the job as well as provides a chance to learn from those already in the business.

Some high school students may gain exposure to automotive repairs through participation in organizations, such as SkillsUSA-Vocational Industrial Clubs of America (VICA). VICA coordinates competitions in several vocational areas, including collision repair. The collision repair competition tests students' aptitudes in metal work, MIG welding, painting, alignment of body and frame, estimation of damage to automobiles, and plastic identification and repair. VICA is represented in all 50 states. If your school does not have a VICA chapter, ask your guidance counselor about starting one or participating in a co-op arrangement with another school.

Employers

Automobile collision repairers hold about 221,000 jobs in the United States. Most work for body shops specializing in body repairs and painting, including private shops and shops operated by automobile dealers. Others work for organizations that maintain their own vehicle fleets, such as trucking companies and automobile rental companies. About one of every six automobile collision repairers is self-employed, operating small shops in cities large and small.

Starting Out

The best way to start out in the field of automobile collision repair is, first, to attend one of the many postsecondary training programs available throughout the country and, second, to obtain certification. Trade and technical schools usually provide job placement assistance for their graduates. Schools often have contacts with local employers who seek highly skilled entry-level employees. Often, employers post job openings at nearby trade schools with accredited programs.

Although postsecondary training programs are considered the best way to enter the field, some repairers learn the trade on the job as apprentices. Their training consists of working for several years under the guidance of experienced repairers. Fewer employers today are willing to hire apprentices because of the time and cost it takes to train them, but since there currently is a shortage of high-quality entry-level collision repair technicians, many employers will continue to hire apprentices who can demonstrate good mechanical aptitude and a willingness to learn. Those who do learn their skills on the job will inevitably require some formal training if they wish to advance and stay in step with the changing industry.

Internship programs sponsored by car manufacturers or independent organizations provide students with excellent opportunities to actually work with prospective employers. Internships can also provide students with valuable contacts who will be able to refer students to future employers and provide a recommendation to potential employers once they have completed their training. Many students may even be hired by the company at which they interned.

Advancement

Like NATEF training programs, currently employed collision repairers may be certified by the ASE. Although certification is voluntary, it is a widely recognized standard of achievement for automobile collision repairers and the way many advance. Collision repairers who are certified are more valuable to their employers than those who are not and therefore stand a greater chance of advancement.

Certification is available in four specialty areas: structural analysis and damage repair, nonstructural analysis and damage repair, mechanical and electrical components, and painting and refinishing. Those who have passed all the exams are certified as master body/paint technicians. To maintain their certification, technicians must retake the examination for their specialties every five years. Many employers will hire only accredited technicians, basing salary on the technician's level of accreditation.

With today's complex automobile components and new materials requiring hundreds of hours of study and practice to master, employers encourage their employees to advance in responsibility by learning new systems and repair procedures. A repair shop's reputation will go only as far as its employees are skilled. Those with good communication and planning skills may advance to shop supervisor or service manager at larger repair shops or dealerships. Those who have mastered collision repair may go on to teaching at postsecondary schools or work for certification agencies.

Earnings

Salary ranges of collision repairers vary depending on level of experience, type of shop, and geographic location. Most earned hourly salaries between $11.12 and $20.02, with a median hourly salary of $15.00 in 2000, according to the U.S. Department of Labor. At the lower end of the pay scale, collision repairers with less experience and repairers who were employed by smaller shops earned about $8.49 per hour in 2000. At the high end of the pay scale, experienced repairers with management positions earned more than $26.06 an hour. In many repair shops and dealerships, collision repairers can earn more by working on commission. They typically earn 40 to 50 percent of the labor costs charged to customers. Employers often guarantee a minimum level of pay in addition to commissions.

Benefits packages vary from business to business. Most repair technicians can expect health insurance and a paid vacation from employers. Other benefits may include dental and eye care, life and disability insurance, and a pension plan. Employers usually cover a technician's work clothes and may pay a percentage of the cost of hand tools a technician purchases. An increasing number of employers pay all or most of an employee's certification training, dependent on the employee passing the test. A technician's salary can increase through yearly bonuses or profit sharing if the business does well.

Work Environment

Collision repair work is generally noisy, dusty, and dirty. In some cases, the noise and dirt levels have decreased as new technology such as computers and electrostatic paint guns are introduced. Automobile repair shops are usually well ventilated to reduce dust and dangerous fumes. Because repairers weld and handle hot or jagged pieces of metal and broken glass, they wear safety glasses, masks, and protective gloves. Minor hand and back injuries are the most common problems of technicians. When reaching in hard-to-get-at places or loosening tight bolts, collision repairers often bruise, cut, or burn their hands. With caution and experience, most learn to avoid hand injuries. Working for long periods in cramped or bent positions often results in a stiff back or neck. Collision repairers also lift many heavy objects that can cause injury if not handled carefully; however, this is less of a problem with new cars, as automakers design smaller and lighter parts for better fuel economy. Automotive painters wear respirators and other protective gear, and they work in specially ventilated rooms to keep from being exposed to paint fumes and other hazardous chemicals. Painters may need to stand for hours at a time as they work.

By following safety procedures and learning how to avoid typical problems, repairers can minimize the risks involved in this job. Likewise, shops must comply with strict safety procedures to help employees avoid accident or injury. Collision repairers are often under pressure to complete the job quickly. Most repairers work a standard 40-hour week but may be required to work longer hours when the shop is busy or in emergencies.

Outlook

Like many service industries, the collision repair industry is facing a labor shortage of skilled, entry-level workers in many areas of the country. Demand for collision repair services is expected to remain consistent, at the least, and employment opportunities are expected to increase about as fast as the average through 2010. This demand, paired with technology that will require new skills, translates into a healthy job market for those willing to undergo the training needed. According to *Automotive Body Repair News*, as the need for skilled labor is rising, the number of people pursuing collision repair careers is declining. In many cases, vocational schools and employers are teaming up to recruit new workers.

Changing technology also plays a role in the industry's outlook. New automobile designs have body parts made of steel alloys, aluminum, and plastics—materials that are more time consuming to work with. In many cases, such materials are more prone to damage, increasing the need for body repairs.

The automobile collision repair business is not greatly affected by changes in economic conditions. Major body damage must be repaired to keep a vehicle in safe operating condition. During an economic downturn, however, people tend to postpone minor repairs until their budgets can accommodate the expense. Nevertheless, body repairers are seldom laid off. Instead, when business is bad, employers hire fewer new workers. During a recession, inexperienced workers face strong competition for entry-level jobs. People with formal training in repair work and automobile mechanics are likely to have the best job prospects in such times.

For More Information

For more information on careers, training, and accreditation, contact the following organizations:

AUTOMOTIVE AFTERMARKET INDUSTRY ASSOCIATION
4600 East-West Highway, Suite 300
Bethesda, MD 20814-3415
Tel: 301-654-6664
Email: aaia@aftermarket.org
Web: http://www.aftermarket.org

INTER-INDUSTRY CONFERENCE ON AUTO COLLISION REPAIR
3701 Algonquin Road, Suite 400
Rolling Meadows, IL 60008
Tel: 800-422-7872
Web: http://www.i-car.com

NATIONAL AUTOMOTIVE TECHNICIANS EDUCATION FOUNDATION
101 Blue Seal Drive, Suite 101
Leesburg, VA 20175
Tel: 703-669-6650
Web: http://www.natef.org

NATIONAL INSTITUTE FOR AUTOMOTIVE SERVICE EXCELLENCE
101 Blue Seal Drive, SE, Suite 101
Leesburg, VA 20175
Tel: 877-273-8324
Web: http://www.asecert.org

Automobile Service Technicians

Quick Facts

School Subjects
  Business
  Technical/shop
Personal Skills
  Mechanical/manipulative
  Technical/scientific
Work Environment
  Primarily indoors
  Primarily one location
Minimum Education Level
  High school diploma
Salary Range
  $15,787 to $28,496 to $100,000
Certification or Licensing
  Recommended
Outlook
  About as fast as the average

Overview

Automobile service technicians maintain and repair cars, vans, small trucks, and other vehicles. Using both hand tools and specialized diagnostic test equipment, they pinpoint problems and make the necessary repairs or adjustments. In addition to performing complex and difficult repairs, technicians perform a number of routine maintenance procedures, such as oil changes, tire rotation, and battery replacement. Technicians interact frequently with customers to explain repair procedures and discuss maintenance needs. Approximately 840,000 automotive service technicians work in the United States.

History

By the mid-1920s, the automobile industry began to change America. As automobiles changed through the years, mechanics—or automobile service technicians, as they are now called—have kept them running. The "Big Three" automobile makers—Ford, General Motors, and Chrysler—produced millions of cars for a public eager for the freedom and mobility the automobile promised. With the ill-prepared roads suddenly overrun by inexperienced drivers, accidents and breakdowns became common. People not only were unskilled in driving but also were ignorant of the basic maintenance and service the automobile required. It suddenly became apparent that a new profession was in the making.

Already in 1899 the American Motor Company opened a garage in New York and advertised "competent mechanics always on hand to make repairs when necessary." Gradually, other repair "garages" opened in larger cities, but they were few and far between. Automobiles were significantly simpler in the early years. Basic maintenance and minor repairs often could be performed by the owner or someone with general mechanical aptitude.

As cars became more complex, the need for qualified technicians grew. Dealerships began to hire mechanics to handle increasing customer concerns and complaints. Gas stations also began to offer repair and maintenance services. The profession of automobile mechanic was suddenly in big demand.

By the 1950s, automobile service and repair garages were common throughout the United States, in urban and rural areas alike. Most mechanics learned the trade through hands-on experience as an apprentice or on their own through trial and error. When automakers began packing their cars with new technology, involving complex electrical circuitry and computer-controlled mechanisms as well as basic design changes, it became apparent that mechanics would need comprehensive training to learn new service and repair procedures. Until the 1970s, there was no standard by which automobile service technicians were trained. In 1972, the National Institute for Automotive Service Excellence (ASE) was established. It set national training standards for new technicians and provided continuing education and certification for existing technicians when new technology became widespread in the field.

Today, the demand for trained, highly skilled professionals in the service industry is greater than ever. To keep up with the technology that is continually incorporated in new vehicles, service technicians need more intensive training than in the past. Today, mechanics who have completed a high level of formal training are generally called automobile service technicians. They have studied the complexities of the latest automotive technology, from computerized mechanisms in the engine to specialized diagnostic testing equipment.

The Job

Many automobile service technicians feel that the most exciting part of their work is troubleshooting—locating the source of a problem and successfully fixing it. Diagnosing mechanical, electrical, and computer-related troubles requires a broad knowledge of how cars work, the ability to make accurate observations, and the patience to logically determine what went wrong. Technicians agree that it frequently is more difficult to find the problem than it is to fix it. With experience, knowing where to look for problems becomes second nature.

Generally, there are two types of automobile service technicians: *generalists* and *specialists.* Generalists work under a broad umbrella of repair and service duties. They have proficiency in several kinds of light repairs and maintenance of many different types of automobiles. Their work, for the most part, is routine and basic. Specialists concentrate in one or two areas and learn to master them for many different car makes and models. Today, in light of the sophisticated technology common in new cars, there is an increasing demand for specialists. Automotive systems are not as easy or as standard as they used to be, and they now require many hours of experience to master. To gain a broad knowledge in auto maintenance and repair, specialists usually begin as generalists.

When a car does not operate properly, the owner brings it to a service technician and describes the problem. At a dealership or larger shop, the customer may talk with a *repair service estimator,* who writes down the customer's description of the problem and relays it to the service technician. The technician may test-drive the car or use diagnostic equipment, such as motor analyzers, spark plug testers, or compression gauges, to determine the problem. If a customer explains that the car's automatic transmission does not shift gears at the right times, the technician must know how the functioning of the transmission depends on the engine vacuum, the throttle pressure, and—more common in newer cars—the onboard computer. Each factor must be thoroughly checked. With each test, clues help the technician pinpoint the cause of the malfunction. After successfully diagnosing the problem, the technician makes the necessary adjustments or repairs. If a part is too badly damaged or worn to be repaired, he or she replaces it after first consulting the car owner, explaining the problem, and estimating the cost.

Normal use of an automobile inevitably causes wear and deterioration of parts. Generalist automobile technicians handle many of the routine maintenance tasks to help keep a car in optimal operating condition. They change oil, lubricate parts, and adjust or replace components of any of the car's systems that might cause a malfunction, including belts, hoses, spark plugs, brakes, filters, and transmission and coolant fluids.

Technicians who specialize in the service of specific parts usually work in large shops with multiple departments, car diagnostic centers, franchised auto service shops, or small independent shops that concentrate on a particular type of repair work.

Tune-up technicians evaluate and correct engine performance and fuel economy. They use diagnostic equipment and other computerized devices to locate malfunctions in fuel, ignition, and emissions-control systems. They adjust ignition timing and valves and may replace spark plugs, points, triggering assemblies in electronic ignitions, and other components to ensure maximum engine efficiency.

Electrical-systems technicians have been in greater demand in recent years. They service and repair the complex electrical and computer circuitry common in today's automobile. They use both sophisticated diagnostic equipment and simpler devices such as ammeters, ohmmeters, and voltmeters to locate system malfunctions. As well as possessing excellent electrical skills, electrical-systems technicians require basic mechanical aptitude to get at electrical and computer circuitry located throughout the automobile.

Front-end technicians are concerned with suspension and steering systems. They inspect, repair, and replace front-end parts such as springs, shock absorbers, and linkage parts such as tie rods and ball joints. They also align and balance wheels.

Brake repairers work on drum and disk braking systems, parking brakes, and their hydraulic systems. They inspect, adjust, remove, repair, and reinstall such items as brake shoes, disk pads, drums, rotors, wheel and master cylinders, and hydraulic fluid lines. Some specialize in both brake and front-end work.

Transmission technicians adjust, repair, and maintain gear trains, couplings, hydraulic pumps, valve bodies, clutch assemblies, and other parts of automatic transmission systems. Transmissions have become complex and highly sophisticated mechanisms in newer model automobiles. Technicians require special training to learn how they function.

Automobile-radiator mechanics clean radiators using caustic solutions. They locate and solder leaks and install new radiator cores. In addition, some radiator mechanics repair car heaters and air conditioners and solder leaks in gas tanks.

Alternative fuel technicians are relatively new additions to the field. This specialty has evolved with the nation's efforts to reduce its dependence on foreign oil by exploring alternative fuels, such as ethanol and electricity.

As more automobiles rely on a variety of electronic components, technicians have become more proficient in the basics of electronics, even if they are not electronics specialists. Electronic controls and instruments are located in nearly all the systems of today's cars. Many previously mechanical functions in automobiles are being replaced by electronics, significantly altering the way repairs are performed. Diagnosing and correcting problems with electronic components often involves the use of specialty tools and computers.

Automobile service technicians use an array of tools in their everyday work, ranging from simple hand tools to computerized diagnostic equipment. Technicians supply their own hand tools at an investment of $6,000 to $25,000 or more, depending on their specialty. It is usually the employer's responsibility to furnish the larger power tools, engine analyzers, and other test equipment.

To maintain and increase their skills and to keep up with new technology, automobile technicians must regularly read service and repair manuals, shop bulletins, and other publications. They must also be willing to take part in training programs given by manufacturers or at vocational schools. Those who have voluntary certification must periodically retake exams to keep their credentials.

Requirements

HIGH SCHOOL

In today's competitive job market, aspiring automobile service technicians need a high school diploma to land a job that offers growth possibilities, a good salary, and challenges. There is a big demand in the automotive service industry to fill entry-level positions with well-trained, highly skilled persons. Technology demands more from the technician than it did 10 years ago.

In high school, students should take automotive and shop classes, mathematics, English, and computer classes. Adjustments and repairs to many car components require the technician to make numerous computations, for which good mathematical skills are essential. Good reading skills are also valuable, as a technician must do a lot of reading to stay competitive in today's job market. English classes will prepare the technician to handle the many volumes of repair manuals and trade journals he or she will need to remain informed. Computer skills are also vital, as computers are now common in most repair shops. They keep track of customers' histories and parts and often detail repair procedures. Use of computers in repair shops will only increase in the future.

POSTSECONDARY TRAINING
Employers today prefer to hire only those who have completed some kind of formal training program in automobile mechanics—usually a minimum of two years. A wide variety of such programs are offered at community colleges and vocational schools, independent organizations, and manufacturers. Many community colleges and vocational schools around the country offer accredited postsecondary education. Postsecondary training programs prepare students through a blend of classroom instruction and hands-on practical experience. They range in length from six months to two years or more, depending on the type of program. Shorter programs usually involve intensive study. Longer programs typically alternate classroom courses with periods of work experience. Some two-year programs include courses on applied mathematics, reading and writing skills, and business practices and lead to an associate's degree.

Some programs are conducted in association with automobile manufacturers. Students combine work experience with hands-on classroom study of up-to-date equipment and new cars provided by manufacturers. In other programs, students alternate time in the classroom with internships in dealerships or service departments. These students may take up to four years to finish their training, but they become familiar with the latest technology and also earn a modest salary.

CERTIFICATION OR LICENSING
One recognized indicator of quality for entry-level technicians is certification by the National Automotive Technicians Education Foundation (NATEF), an affiliate of the ASE. The NATEF's goals are to develop, encourage, and improve automotive technical education for students seeking entry-level positions as automobile service technicians. The NATEF certifies many postsecondary programs for training throughout the country. Certification is available in the areas of automatic transmission/transaxle, brakes, electrical systems, engine performance, engine repair, heating and air conditioning, manual drive train and axles, and suspension and steering. Certification assures students that the program they enroll in meets the standards employers expect from their entry-level employees. ASE certification is not required, but job applicants who are certified certainly have a competitive advantage over those who are not.

OTHER REQUIREMENTS

Automobile service technicians must be patient and thorough in their work; a shoddy repair job may put the driver's life at risk. They must have excellent troubleshooting skills and be able to logically deduce the cause of system malfunctions.

Exploring

Many community centers offer general auto maintenance and mechanics workshops where students can practice working on cars and learn from instructors. Trade magazines are excellent sources for learning what's new in the industry and can be found at most public libraries or large bookstores. Many public television stations broadcast automobile maintenance and repair programs that can be of help to beginners to see how various types of cars differ.

Working on cars as a hobby provides valuable firsthand experience in the work of a technician. An after-school or weekend part-time job in a repair shop or dealership can give a feel for the general atmosphere and kinds of problems technicians face on the job. Oil and tire changes, battery and belt replacement, and even pumping gas may be some of the things part-timers are required to do on the job, but this is valuable experience that is necessary before moving on to more complex repairs. Experience with vehicle repair work in the armed forces is another way many people pursue their interest in this field.

Employers

Because the automotive industry is so vast, automobile service technicians have many choices concerning type of shop and geographic location. Automobile repairs are needed all over the country, in large cities as well as rural areas.

The majority of automobile service technicians work for automotive dealers and independent automotive repair shops and gasoline service stations. The field offers a variety of other employment options as well. The U.S. Department of Labor estimates that 18 percent of automobile service technicians are self-employed. Other employers include franchises such as Pep Boys and Midas that offer routine repairs and maintenance, and automotive service departments of automotive and home supply stores. Some automobile service technicians maintain fleets for taxicab and automobile leasing companies or for government agencies with large automobile fleets.

Technicians with experience and/or ASE certification certainly have more career choices. Some master mechanics may go on to teach at technical and vocational schools or at community colleges. Others put in many years working for someone else and go into business for themselves after they have gained the experience to handle many types of repairs and oversee other technicians.

Starting Out

The best way to start out in this field is to attend one of the many post-secondary training programs available throughout the country and obtain accreditation. Trade and technical schools usually provide job placement assistance for their graduates. Schools often have contacts with local employers who need to hire well-trained people. Frequently, employers post job openings at nearby trade schools with accredited programs. Job openings are frequently listed on the Internet through regional and national automotive associations or career networks.

A decreasing number of technicians learn the trade on the job as apprentices. Their training consists of working for several years under the guidance of experienced mechanics. Fewer employers today are willing to hire apprentices due to the time and money it takes to train them. Those who do learn their skills on the job will inevitably require some formal training if they wish to advance and stay in step with the changing industry.

Intern programs sponsored by car manufacturers or independent organizations provide students with excellent opportunities to actually work with prospective employers. Internships can provide students with valuable contacts who will be able to recommend future employers once students have completed their training. Many students may even be hired by the shop at which they interned.

Advancement

Currently employed technicians may be certified by the ASE in eight different areas. Those who become certified in all eight areas are known as master mechanics. Although certification is voluntary, it is a widely recognized standard of achievement for automobile technicians and is highly valued by many employers. Certification also provides the means and opportunity to advance. To maintain their certification, technicians must retake the examination for their specialties every five years. Many employers hire only ASE-accredited technicians and base salaries on the level of the technicians' accreditation.

With today's complex automobile components requiring hundreds of hours of study and practice to master, more repair shops prefer to hire specialists. Generalist automobile technicians advance as they gain experience and become specialists. Other technicians advance to diesel repair, where the pay may be higher. Those with good communication and planning skills may advance to shop foreman or service manager at large repair shops or to sales workers at dealerships. Master mechanics with good business skills often go into business for themselves and open their own shops.

Earnings

Salary ranges of automobile service technicians vary depending on the level of experience, the type of shop the technician works in, and geographic location. Generally, technicians who work in small-town, family-owned gas stations earn less than those who work at dealerships and franchises in metropolitan areas.

According to the U.S. Department of Labor, the lowest-paid automobile service technicians earned about $7.59 per hour (or $15,787 annually) in 2000. The median hourly salary for automobile service technicians was $13.70 (or $28,496 annually) in 2000. Top-paid technicians with experience and certification earned more than $23.67 per hour (or $49,234+ annually) in 2000. Since most technicians work on an hourly basis and frequently work overtime, their salaries can vary significantly. In many repair shops and dealerships, technicians can earn higher incomes by working on commission. In 2001, master technicians who worked on commission were reported to have earned between $70,000 and $100,000 annually. Employers often guarantee a minimum level of pay in addition to commissions.

Benefit packages vary from business to business. Most technicians can expect health insurance and paid vacation days. Additional benefits may include dental, life, and disability insurance and a pension plan. Employers usually cover a technician's work clothes and may pay a percentage on hand tools purchased. An increasing number of employers pay all or most of an employee's certification training, if he or she passes the test. A technician's salary can increase through yearly bonuses or profit sharing if the business does well.

Work Environment

Depending on the size of the shop and whether it's an independent or franchised repair shop, dealership, or private business, automobile technicians work with anywhere from two to 20 other technicians. Most shops are well lighted and well ventilated. They can frequently be noisy with running cars and power tools. Minor hand and back injuries are the most common problems of technicians. When reaching in hard-to-get-at places or loosening tight bolts, technicians often bruise, cut, or burn their hands. With caution and experience, most technicians learn to avoid hand injuries. Working for long periods of time in cramped or bent positions often results in a stiff back or neck. Technicians also lift many heavy objects that can cause injury if not handled carefully; however, this is becoming less of a problem with new cars, as automakers design smaller and lighter parts to improve fuel economy. Some technicians may experience allergic reactions to solvents and oils used in cleaning, maintenance, and repair. Shops must comply with strict safety procedures set by the Occupational Safety Hazard Administration and Environmental Protection Agency to help employees avoid accidents and injuries.

The U.S. Department of Labor reports that most technicians work a standard 40-hour week, but 30 percent of all technicians work more than 40 hours a week. Some technicians make emergency repairs to stranded automobiles on the roadside during odd hours.

Outlook

With an estimated 189 million vehicles in operation today, automobile service technicians should feel confident that a good percentage will require servicing and repair. Skilled and highly trained technicians will be in particular demand. Less-skilled workers will face tough competition. The U.S. Department of Labor predicts that this field will grow as fast as the average through 2010, but in some areas, growth could be higher because of a tight labor market. According to the ASE, even if school enrollments were at maximum capacity, the demand for automobile service technicians still would exceed the supply in the immediate future. As a result, many shops are beginning to recruit employees while they are still in vocational or even high school.

Another concern for the industry is the automobile industry's trend toward developing the "maintenance-free" car. Manufacturers are producing high-end cars that require no servicing for their first 100,000 miles. In addition, many new cars are equipped with on-board diagnostics that detect both wear and failure for many of the car's components, eliminating the need for technicians to perform extensive diagnostic tests. Also, parts that are replaced before they completely wear out prevent further damage from occurring to connected parts that are affected by a malfunction or breakdown. Although this will reduce troubleshooting time and the number of overall repairs, the components that need repair will be more costly and require a more experienced (and hence, more expensive) technician.

Most new jobs for technicians will be at independent service dealers, specialty shops, and franchised new car dealers. Because of the increase of specialty shops, fewer gasoline service stations will hire technicians, and many will eliminate repair services completely. Other opportunities will be available at companies or institutions with private fleets (e.g., cab, delivery, and rental companies, and government agencies and police departments).

For More Information

For more information on the automotive service industry, contact the following organizations:

AUTOMOTIVE AFTERMARKET INDUSTRY ASSOCIATION
4600 East-West Highway, Suite 300
Bethesda, MD 20814-3415
Tel: 301-654-6664
Email: aaia@aftermarket.org
Web: http://www.aftermarket.org

AUTOMOTIVE SERVICE ASSOCIATION
PO Box 929
Bedford, TX 76095-0929
Tel: 800-272-7467
Email: asainfo@asashop.org
Web: http://www.asashop.org

NATIONAL AUTOMOBILE DEALERS ASSOCIATION
8400 Westpark Drive
McLean, VA 22102
Tel: 800-252-6232
Email: nadainfo@nada.org
Web: http://www.nada.org

NATIONAL AUTOMOTIVE TECHNICIANS EDUCATION FOUNDATION
101 Blue Seal Drive, Suite 101
Leesburg, VA 20175
Tel: 703-669-6650
Web: http://www.natef.org

For information on certification, contact:
NATIONAL INSTITUTE FOR AUTOMOTIVE SERVICE EXCELLENCE
101 Blue Seal Drive, SE, Suite 101
Leesburg, VA 20175
Tel: 877-273-8324
Web: http://www.asecert.org

Bicycle Mechanics

Quick Facts

School Subjects
Mathematics
Physics
Technical/shop

Personal Skills
Following instructions
Mechanical/manipulative

Work Environment
Primarily indoors
Primarily one location

Minimum Education Level
High school diploma

Salary Range
$10,400 to $16,640 to $25,220

Certification or Licensing
Voluntary

Outlook
About as fast as the average

Overview

Bicycle mechanics use hand and power tools to repair, service, and assemble all types of bicycles. They may do routine maintenance and tune-ups or completely rebuild damaged or old bicycles. Bike manufacturers, dealers, retail bike and sporting goods stores, and general merchandise stores may employ bicycle mechanics. The popularity of bicycles and the fact that many riders lack the time to repair their bikes make for a steady employment outlook for bicycle mechanics. Approximately 8,500 bicycle mechanics work in the United States.

History

Bicycles have been said to be the most efficient means ever devised to turn human energy into propulsion. The first successful bicycle was built in Scotland around 1839. It, like the bicycles built for many years afterward, had a large front wheel that was pedaled and steered and a smaller wheel in back for balance. In time, advances in design and technology improved the ease with which riders could balance, steer, brake, and get on and off bicycles. The first modern-looking bicycle, with equal-sized front and rear wheels and a loop of chain on a sprocket drive, was built in 1874. By the early 1890s, pneumatic tires and the basic diamond-pattern frame made bicycles stable, efficient, and fairly inexpensive. Bicycle riding became a popular recreation and, in some countries around the world, a major form of transportation. In the 20th century, bicycle performance was further improved by lightweight frames with new designs and improved gear mechanisms, tires, and other components.

After automobiles became the dominant vehicles on American roads, bicycles were usually considered children's toys in the United States. However, the 1960s and 1970s saw a resurgence in their popularity among adults that has continued to this day. With the increasing costs associated with cars and environmental concerns, more people are using bikes, not only for exercise, racing, or touring, but also for short trips to the store, to visit friends, or to go to work.

The Job

Repairing bicycles takes mechanical skill and careful attention to detail. Many repairs, such as replacing brake cables, are relatively simple, while others can be very complicated. Mechanics use a variety of tools, including wrenches, screwdrivers, drills, vises, and specialized tools, to repair and maintain bikes. There are many different brands of bikes, both domestic and foreign, and each has its own unique characteristics and mechanical problems.

Bicycle mechanics work on both new and used bicycles. They may be required to do emergency repairs or routine tune-ups, or they may need to repair and recondition used bikes so they can be sold. Many new bikes come from the manufacturer unassembled, and mechanics working at a bicycle dealership or shop must assemble them and make adjustments so they operate properly. Many department stores and discount houses that sell bikes contract out this type of assembly work to dealerships or bike shops, and it can be very profitable.

Some of the basic repairs that bicycles need can easily be done by the owner, but many cyclists lack the tools, time, or initiative to learn how to service their bikes. They prefer to take most problems to professional bicycle mechanics. One type of repair is fixing a flat tire. Leaks in *clincher tires* (those with a separate inner tube) can be fixed at home, but many owners choose to take them to a bicycle mechanic. Repairing *sew-up tires* (which have no inner tube) is a more complicated process that generally requires a mechanic. Mechanics can also build wheels, replace and tighten spokes, and "true," or align, the wheels. To build a wheel, the mechanic laces the spokes between the rim and the hub of the wheel and then tightens them individually with a special wrench until the wheel spins without wobbling. A truing machine is used to test the balance of the wheel as it spins.

The gear mechanism on multiple-speed bikes is another common concern for bicycle mechanics. On some bikes, gears are shifted by means of a derailleur, which is located on the back wheel hub or at the bottom bracket assembly where the pedals and chain meet. This derailleur frequently needs adjustment. The mechanic aligns the front and rear gears of the derailleur to reduce wear on both the chain and the gear teeth and adjusts the mechanism to keep constant pressure on the chain. Gear mechanisms vary greatly among different makes of bicycles, so mechanics have to keep up with current models and trends.

Bicycle mechanics must be able to spot trouble in a bike and correct problems before they become serious. They may have to straighten a bent frame by using a special vise and a heavy steel rod. They may be asked to adjust or replace the braking mechanism so that the force on the brakes is spread evenly. They may need to take apart, clean, grease, and reassemble the headset, or front hub, and the bottom bracket that houses the axle of the pedal crank.

Mechanics who work in a bike shop sometimes work as salespeople, advising customers on their bike purchases or accessories, including helmets, clothing, mirrors, locks, racks, bags, and more. In some shops, especially those located in resort areas, bike mechanics may also work as bicycle-rental clerks. Where winters are cold and biking is seasonal, bike mechanics may work part of the year on other recreational equipment, such as fitness equipment, snowmobiles, or small engines.

Requirements

HIGH SCHOOL

Completion of high school or other formal education is not necessarily required for a job as a bicycle mechanic, although employers may prefer applicants who are high school graduates. If you are considering this kind of work, you will benefit from taking vocational-technical or shop classes in high school. Such classes will give you the opportunity to work with your hands, follow blueprints or other directions, and build equipment. Science classes, such as physics, will give you an understanding of the principles at work behind the design of equipment as well as help you to understand how it functions. Since you will most likely be working in a retail environment, consider taking business, accounting, or computer classes that will give you business skills. Don't forget to take English or communication classes. These classes will help you develop your communication skills, an asset when dealing with customers, as well as your research and reading skills, an asset when your work includes reviewing maintenance and repair documentation for many different types of bikes.

CERTIFICATION OR LICENSING

Bicycle maintenance courses are offered at some technical and vocational schools, and there are at least three privately operated training schools for mechanics. Bicycle manufacturers may also offer factory instruction to mechanics employed by the company's authorized dealers. Completion of many of the courses offered earns the mechanic certificates that may help when seeking a job or when seeking a promotion.

OTHER REQUIREMENTS

For the most part, bicycle mechanics learn informally on the job. At least two years of hands-on training and experience is required to become a thoroughly skilled mechanic, but because new makes and models of bikes are constantly being introduced, there are always new things to learn that may require additional training. Many times a bicycle distributor visits bike mechanics at a shop to make sure the mechanic's work is competent before the shop is officially permitted to sell and service a new kind of bike. Because of this steady stream of new information, bicycle mechanics must have a desire to study and add to their knowledge.

Bicycle mechanics also need excellent hand-eye coordination and a certain degree of physical endurance. They may work with small tools to make fine adjustments. Often much of their work is performed while they stand, bend, or kneel. Mechanics must be independent decision makers, able to decide on proper repair strategies, but they should also be able to work comfortably with others. Frequently they will need to interact with customers and other workers.

Exploring

Many people become interested in bicycle repair because they own and maintain their own bikes. Taking general maintenance and tune-up classes that some bike shops offer for bicycle owners is a good way for you to explore your interest in working with bikes. Visit with the bicycle mechanics at these shops and ask them for their insights. How did they start in this line of work? What do they enjoy most about it? What is the most challenging aspect of the job? If a local shop does not offer classes, consider taking courses at a private school such as the United Bicycle Institute or the Barnett Bicycle Institute (contact information is at the end of this article).

Bike shops sometimes hire inexperienced students as assistants to work on a part-time basis or during the summer, when their business is most brisk. Such a job is probably the best way to find out about this type of work.

There are various magazines available at larger newsstands, bookstores, or public libraries that are devoted to recreational cycling and serious bicycle racing. These magazines often include the technical aspects of how bicycles are constructed and operated, and they may provide helpful information to anyone interested in bike repair. Bicycle associations can provide additional information regarding classes, industry news, and employment.

Employers

There are approximately 8,500 bicycle mechanics working in the United States, and they are employed nationwide. They may work in local bicycle shops, for large sporting goods stores, or for bicycle manufacturers. Resorts and some retail stores also hire people with these skills. Bicycle mechanics may also be required to repair other types of equipment or serve as sales clerks.

Starting Out

If you are a beginner with no experience, start out by contacting local bike shops or bike manufacturers to find one that is willing to hire trainees. Check the Yellow Pages for a list of bicycle dealers in your area. Bike dealers may also be willing to provide on-the-job training. In addition, the want ads of your local newspaper are a source of information on job openings. Also, try joining a local bicycling club that will allow you to network with other enthusiasts who may know of open positions.

People who have learned bike repair and have accumulated the tools they need may be able to do repair work independently, perhaps using ads and referrals to gradually build a small business.

Advancement

There are few opportunities for advancement for bicycle mechanics unless they combine their interest in bikes with another activity. For example, after a few years on the job, they may be able to start managing the bike shop where they work. Some mechanics move on to jobs with the bicycle department of a large department or sporting goods store and from there move up to department manager or regional sales manager. Another possibility is to become a sales representative for a bicycle manufacturer or distributor.

Some bicycle mechanics want to own and operate their own bike stores. If they gain enough experience and save or borrow enough money to cover start-up costs, they may be able to establish a successful new business. College courses in business, management, and accounting are recommended for aspiring shop owners.

Earnings

Many bicycle mechanics work a standard 40-hour week. In some areas of the country, mechanics may find that their hours increase in the spring, when people bring their bikes out of storage, and decrease when the weather gets colder. Workers in this field are typically paid on an hourly basis.

Trainee mechanics, with less than one year's experience, may start at $5 to $6 per hour, which translates into $10,400 to $12,480 annually. As they gain more experience and become more valuable to their employers, mechanics may make $8 to $9 hourly, or $16,640 to $18,720 a year. According to *The O*Net Dictionary of Occupational Titles*, mechanics who also have sales responsibilities had an annual income of approximately $25,220.

Benefits vary depending on the shop or facility and the number of hours worked. Some jobs may include standard benefits.

Work Environment

Bicycle mechanics do much of their work indoors standing at a workbench. They work constantly with their hands and various tools to perform the prescribed tasks. It is a job that requires attention to detail and, in some cases, the ability to diagnose and troubleshoot problems.

Because of the wide variety of bicycles on the market today, mechanics must be familiar with many different types of bicycles and their problems and repair procedures. Although it is sometimes greasy and dirty work, it is, in general, not very strenuous. Most heavy work, such as painting, brazing, and frame straightening, is done in larger bike shops and specialty shops.

Once the job is mastered, workers may find it somewhat repetitious and not very challenging. It may also be frustrating in cases where bicycles are so old or in such bad shape that they are virtually irreparable. Most often, bicycle mechanics choose this profession because they are cycling enthusiasts themselves. If this is the case, it may be very enjoyable for them to be able to work with bicycles and interact with customers who are fellow cyclists.

Mechanics work by themselves or with a few co-workers as they service bikes, but in many shops they also deal with the public, working the register or helping customers select and purchase bicycles and accessories. The atmosphere around a bike shop can be hectic, especially during peak seasons in shops where mechanics must double as clerks. As is true in any retail situation, bicycle mechanics may sometimes have to deal with irate or rude customers.

Outlook

Cycling continues to gain in popularity. People are bicycling for fun, for fitness, as a means of transportation, and for the thrill of racing. Bikes don't burn gas or pollute the atmosphere, and they are relatively cheap and versatile. With personal fitness and the preservation of the environment as two of the nation's biggest trends and concerns, the bicycling industry looks to a positive future. The U.S. Department of Labor predicts employment for bicycle mechanics to grow about as fast as the average through 2010.

Bicycle repair work is also relatively immune to fluctuations in the economy. In times of economic boom, people buy more new bikes, and mechanics are kept busy assembling, selling, and servicing them. During economic recessions, people take their old bikes to mechanics for repair.

For More Information

For biking news and to read online articles from the magazine
Adventure Cyclist, *contact:*
ADVENTURE CYCLING ASSOCIATION
150 East Pine Street
PO Box 8308
Missoula, MT 59807
Email: info@adventurecycling.org
Web: http://www.adv-cycling.org

For information on courses in bicycle repair and mechanics, contact:
BARNETT BICYCLE INSTITUTE
2755 Ore Mill Drive, Number 14
Colorado Springs, CO 80904
Web: http://www.bbinstitute.com

For news and information about upcoming races and events, contact:
LEAGUE OF AMERICAN BICYCLISTS
1612 K Street, NW, Suite 800
Washington, DC 20006-2082
Email: bikeleague@bikeleague.org
Web: http://www.bikeleague.org

For more information on the industry, contact:
NATIONAL BICYCLE DEALERS ASSOCIATION
777 West 19th Street, Suite O
Costa Mesa, CA 92627
Web: http://www.nbda.com

*For information on beginning to advanced courses in repair, frame
building, and mechanic certification, contact:*
UNITED BICYCLE INSTITUTE
401 Williamson Way
PO Box 128
Ashland, OR 97520
Email: info@bikeschool.com
Web: http://www.bikeschool.com

Biomedical Equipment Technicians

Quick Facts

School Subjects
Biology
Technical/shop
Personal Skills
Mechanical/manipulative
Technical/scientific
Work Environment
Primarily indoors
Primarily one location
Minimum Education Level
Associate's degree
Salary Range
$20,000 to $35,340 to $44,000
Certification or Licensing
Recommended
Outlook
About as fast as the average

Overview

Biomedical equipment technicians handle the complex medical equipment and instruments found in hospitals, clinics, and research facilities. This equipment is used for medical therapy and diagnosis and includes heart-lung machines, artificial kidney machines, patient monitors, chemical analyzers, and other electrical, electronic, mechanical, or pneumatic devices.

Technicians' main duties are to inspect, maintain, repair, and install this equipment. They disassemble equipment to locate malfunctioning components, repair or replace defective parts, and reassemble the equipment, adjusting and calibrating it to ensure that it operates according to manufacturers' specifications. Other duties of biomedical equipment technicians include modifying equipment according to the directions of medical or supervisory personnel, arranging with equipment manufacturers for necessary equipment repair, and safety-testing equipment to ensure that patients, equipment operators, and other staff members are safe from electrical or mechanical hazards. Biomedical equipment technicians work with hand tools, power tools, measuring devices, and manufacturers' manuals.

Technicians may work for equipment manufacturers as salespeople or as service technicians, or for a health care facility specializing in the repair or maintenance of specific equipment, such as that used in radiology, nuclear medicine, or patient monitoring. In the United States, approximately 28,000 people work as biomedical equipment technicians.

History

Today's complex biomedical equipment is the result of advances in three different areas of engineering and scientific research. The first, of course, is our ever-increasing knowledge of the human body and of the disease processes that afflict it. Although the accumulation of medical knowledge has been going on for thousands of years, most of the discoveries leading to the development of medical technology have occurred during the last 300 years. During the past 100 years especially, we have learned a great deal about the chemical and electrical nature of the human body.

The second contribution to biomedical technology's development is the field of instrumentation—the design and building of precision measuring devices. Throughout the history of medicine, physicians and medical researchers have tried to learn about and to monitor the workings of the human body with whatever instruments were available to them. However, it was not until the Industrial Revolution of the 18th and 19th centuries that instruments were developed that could detect the human body's many subtle and rapid processes.

The third area is mechanization and automation. Biomedical equipment often relies on mechanisms, such as pumps, motors, bellows, control arms, etc. These kinds of equipment were initially developed and improved during the Industrial Revolution; however, it was not until the 1950s that the field of medical technology began incorporating the use of automation. During the 1950s, researchers developed machines for analyzing the various components of blood and for preparing tissue specimens for microscopic examination. Probably the most dramatic development of this period was the introduction of the heart-lung machine by John Haysham Gibbon of Philadelphia in 1953, a project he had been working on since 1937.

Since the 1950s, the growth of biomedical technology has been especially dramatic. Thirty years ago, even the most advanced hospitals had only a few pieces of electronic medical equipment; today such hospitals have thousands. And, to service this equipment, the biomedical equipment technician has become an important member of the health care delivery team.

In a sense, biomedical equipment technicians represent the newest stage in the history of technicians. The first technicians were skilled assistants who had learned a trade and gone to work for an engineer or scientist. The second generation learned a technology, such as electronics. The most recent generation of technicians needs integrated instruction and competence in at least two fields of science and technology. For the biomedical equipment technician, the fields may vary, but they will most often be electronics and human physiology.

The Job

Biomedical equipment technicians are an important link between technology and medicine. They repair, calibrate, maintain, and operate biomedical equipment working under the supervision of researchers, biomedical engineers, physicians, surgeons, and other professional health care providers.

Biomedical equipment technicians may work with thousands of different kinds of equipment. Some of the most frequently encountered are patient monitors; heart-lung machines; kidney machines; blood-gas analyzers; spectrophotometers; X-ray units; radiation monitors; defibrillators; anesthesia apparatus; pacemakers; blood pressure transducers; spirometers; sterilizers; diathermy equipment; patient-care computers; ultrasound machines; and diagnostic scanning machines, such as the CT (computed tomography) scan machine, PETT (positive emission transaxial tomography) scanner, and MRI (magnetic resonance imaging) machines.

Repairing faulty instruments is one of the chief functions of biomedical equipment technicians. They investigate equipment problems, determine the extent of malfunctions, make repairs on instruments that have had minor breakdowns, and expedite the repair of instruments with major breakdowns, for instance, by writing an analysis of the problem for the factory. In doing this work, technicians rely on manufacturers' diagrams, maintenance manuals, and standard and specialized test instruments, such as oscilloscopes and pressure gauges.

Installing equipment is another important function of biomedical equipment technicians. They inspect and test new equipment to make sure it complies with performance and safety standards as described in the manufacturer's manuals and diagrams and as noted on the purchase order. Technicians may also check on proper installation of the equipment, or, in some cases, install it themselves. To ensure safe operations, technicians need a thorough knowledge of the regulations related to the proper grounding of equipment, and they need to actively carry out all steps and procedures to ensure safety.

Maintenance is the third major area of responsibility for biomedical equipment technicians. In doing this work, technicians try to catch problems before they become more serious. To this end, they take apart and reassemble devices, test circuits, clean and oil moving parts, and replace worn parts. They also keep complete records of all machine repairs, maintenance checks, and expenses.

In all three of these areas, a large part of technicians' work consists of consulting with physicians, administrators, engineers, and other related professionals. For example, they may be called upon to assist hospital administrators in making decisions about the repair, replacement, or purchase of new equipment. They consult with medical and research staffs to determine that equipment is functioning safely and properly. They also consult with medical and engineering staffs when called upon to modify or develop equipment. In all these activities, technicians use their knowledge of electronics, medical terminology, human anatomy and physiology, chemistry, and physics.

In addition, biomedical equipment technicians are involved in a range of other related duties. Some biomedical equipment technicians maintain inventories of all instruments in the hospital, their condition, location, and operators. They reorder parts and components, assist in providing people with emergency instruments, restore unsafe or defective instruments to working order, and check for safety regulation compliance.

Other biomedical equipment technicians help physicians, surgeons, nurses, and researchers conduct procedures and experiments. In addition, they must be able to explain to staff members how to operate these machines, the conditions under which certain apparatus may or may not be used, how to solve small operating problems, and how to monitor and maintain equipment.

In many hospitals, technicians are assigned to a particular service, such as pediatrics, surgery, or renal medicine. These technicians become specialists in certain types of equipment. However, unlike electrocardiograph technicians or dialysis technicians, who specialize in one kind of equipment, most biomedical equipment technicians must be thoroughly familiar with a large variety of instruments. They might be called upon to prepare an artificial kidney or to work with a blood-gas analyzer. Biomedical equipment technicians also maintain pulmonary function machines. These machines are used in clinics for ambulatory patients, hospital laboratories, departments of medicine for diagnosis and treatment, and rehabilitation of cardiopulmonary patients.

While most biomedical equipment technicians are trained in electronics technology, there is also a need for technicians trained in plastics to work on the development of artificial organs and for people trained in glass blowing to help make the precision parts for specialized equipment.

Many biomedical equipment technicians work for medical instrument manufacturers. These technicians consult and assist in the construction of new machinery, helping to make decisions concerning materials and construction methods to be used in the manufacture of the equipment.

Requirements

HIGH SCHOOL
There are a number of classes you can take in high school to help you prepare for this work. Science classes, such as chemistry, biology, and physics, will give you the science background you will need for working in a medical environment. Take shop classes that deal with electronics, drafting, or blueprint reading. These classes will give you experience working with your hands, following printed directions, using electricity, and working with machinery. Mathematics classes will help you become comfortable working with numbers and formulas. Don't neglect your English studies. English classes will help you develop your communication skills, which will be important to have when you deal with a variety of different people in your professional life.

POSTSECONDARY TRAINING
To become qualified for this work, you will need to complete postsecondary education that leads either to an associate's degree from a two-year institution or to a bachelor's degree from a four-year college or university. Most biomedical equipment technicians choose to receive an associate's degree. Biomedical equipment technology is a relatively new program in some schools and may also be referred to as *medical electronics technology* or *biomedical engineering technology*. No matter

what the name of the program, however, you should expect to receive instruction in such areas as anatomy, physiology, electrical and electronic fundamentals, chemistry, physics, and biomedical equipment construction and design. In addition, you will study safety methods in health care facilities and medical equipment troubleshooting, as it will be your job to be the problem solver. You should also expect to continue taking communications or English classes, since communication skills will be essential to your work. In addition to the classroom work, many programs often provide you with practical experience in repairing and servicing equipment in a clinical or laboratory setting under the supervision of an experienced equipment technician. In this way, you learn about electrical components and circuits, the design and construction of common pieces of machinery, and computer technology as it applies to biomedical equipment.

By studying various pieces of equipment, you learn a problem-solving technique that applies not only to the equipment studied but also to equipment you have not yet seen, and even to equipment that has not yet been invented. Part of this problem-solving technique includes learning how and where to locate sources of information.

Some biomedical equipment technicians receive their training in the armed forces. During the course of an enlistment period of four years or less, military personnel can receive training that prepares them for entry-level or sometimes advanced-level positions in the civilian workforce.

CERTIFICATION OR LICENSING

The Association for the Advancement of Medical Instrumentation (AAMI), affiliated with the International Certification Commission for Clinical Engineering and Biomedical Technology, issues a certificate for biomedical equipment technicians (called CBET) that is based on a written examination, work experience, and educational preparation. In some cases, the educational requirements for certification may be waived for technicians with appropriate employment experience. Although certification is not required for employment, it is highly recommended. Technicians with certification have demonstrated that they have attained an overall knowledge of the field and are dedicated to their profession. Many employers prefer to hire technicians who have this certification.

OTHER REQUIREMENTS

Biomedical equipment technicians need mechanical ability and should enjoy working with tools. Because this job demands quick decision-making and prompt repairs, technicians should work well under pressure. You should also be extremely precise and accurate in your work, have good communication skills, and enjoy helping others—an essential quality for anyone working in the health care industry.

Exploring

You will have difficulty gaining any direct experience in biomedical equipment technology until you are in a training program or working professionally. Your first hands-on opportunities generally come in the clinical and laboratory phases of your education. You can, however, visit school and community libraries to seek out books written about careers in medical technology. You can also join a hobby club devoted to chemistry, biology, radio equipment, or electronics.

Perhaps the best way to learn more about this job is to set up, with the help of teachers or guidance counselors, a visit to a local health care facility or to arrange for a biomedical technician to speak to interested students, either on-site or at a career exploration seminar hosted by the school. You may be able to ask the technician about his or her educational background, what a day on the job is like, and what new technologies are on the horizon. Try to visit a school offering a program in biomedical equipment technology, and discuss your career plans with an admissions counselor there. The counselor may also be able to provide you with helpful insights about the career and your preparation for it.

Finally, because this work involves the health care field, consider getting a part-time job or volunteering at a local hospital. Naturally, you won't be asked to work with the biomedical equipment, but you will have the opportunity to see professionals on the job and experience being in the medical environment. Even if your duty is only to escort patients to their tests, you may gain a greater understanding of this work.

Employers

Many schools place students in part-time hospital positions to help them gain practical experience. Students are often able to return to these hospitals for full-time employment after graduation. Other places of employment include research institutes and biomedical equipment manufacturers. Government hospitals and the military are also employers of biomedical equipment technicians.

Starting Out

Most schools offering programs in biomedical equipment technology work closely with local hospitals and industries, and school placement officers are usually informed about openings when they become available. In some cases, recruiters may visit a school periodically to conduct interviews. Also, many schools place students in part-time hospital jobs to help them gain practical experience. Students are often able to return to these hospitals for full-time employment after graduation.

Another effective method of finding employment is to write directly to hospitals, research institutes, or biomedical equipment manufacturers. Other good sources of leads for job openings include state employment offices and newspaper want ads.

Advancement

With experience, biomedical equipment technicians can expect to work with less supervision, and in some cases they may find themselves supervising less-experienced technicians. They may advance to positions in which they serve as instructors, assist in research, or have administrative duties. Although many supervisory positions are open to biomedical equipment technicians, some positions are not available without additional education. In large metropolitan hospitals, for instance, the minimum educational requirement for biomedical engineers, who do much of the supervising of biomedical equipment technicians, is a bachelor's degree; many engineers have a master's degree as well.

Earnings

Salaries for biomedical equipment technicians vary in different institutions and localities and according to the experience, training, certification, and type of work done by the technician. According to the U.S. Department of Labor, the median hourly wage for medical equipment repairers was $16.99 in 2000. A technician earning this amount and working full time would have a yearly salary of approximately $35,340. A

March 2000 AAMI survey of schools providing biomedical equipment training contains salary figures for their graduates. The average annual salary for those who had graduated from the two-year programs listed in the survey was approximately $28,200. At the low end of the salary ranges provided by these schools, graduates had yearly earnings of $20,000; at the high end of the salary ranges, some graduates reported earnings of $44,000. In general, biomedical equipment technicians who work for manufacturers have higher earnings than those who work for hospitals. Naturally, those in supervisory or senior positions also command higher salaries. Benefits, such as health insurance and vacation days, vary with the employer.

Work Environment

Working conditions for biomedical equipment technicians vary according to employer and type of work done. Hospital employees generally work a 40-hour week; their schedules sometimes include weekends and holidays, and some technicians may be on call for emergencies. Technicians working for equipment manufacturers may have to do extensive traveling to install or service equipment.

The physical surroundings in which biomedical equipment technicians work may vary from day to day. Technicians may work in a lab or treatment room with patients or consult with engineers, administrators, and other staff members. Other days, technicians may spend most of their time at a workbench repairing equipment.

Outlook

Because of the increasing use of electronic medical devices and other sophisticated biomedical equipment, there is a steady demand for skilled and trained biomedical equipment technicians. The U.S. Department of Labor predicts employment for this group to grow about as fast as the average through 2010.

In hospitals, the need for more biomedical equipment technicians exists not only because of the increasing use of biomedical equipment but also because hospital administrators realize that these technicians can help hold down costs. Biomedical equipment technicians do this through their preventive maintenance checks and by taking over some routine activities of engineers and administrators, thus releasing those professionals for activities that only they can perform. Through the coming decades, cost containment will remain a high priority for hospital administrators, and as long as biomedical equipment technicians can contribute to that effort, the demand for them should remain strong.

For the many biomedical equipment technicians who work for companies that build, sell, lease, or service biomedical equipment, job opportunities should also continue to grow.

The federal government employs biomedical equipment technicians in its hospitals, research institutes, and the military. Employment in these areas will depend largely on levels of government spending. In the research area, spending levels may vary; however, in health care delivery, spending should remain high for the near future.

For More Information

For information on student memberships, biomedical technology programs, and certification, contact:

ASSOCIATION FOR THE ADVANCEMENT OF MEDICAL INSTRUMENTATION
1110 North Glebe Road, Suite 220
Arlington, VA 22201-4795
Tel: 800-332-2264
Web: http://www.aami.org

Boilermakers and Boilermaker Mechanics

Quick Facts

School Subjects
  Mathematics
  Technical/shop
Personal Skills
  Mechanical/manipulative
  Technical/scientific
Work Environment
  Indoors and outdoors
  Primarily multiple locations
Minimum Education Level
  Apprenticeship
Salary Range
  $19,970 to $37,024 to $55,765+
Certification or Licensing
  None available
Outlook
  Little change or more slowly than
  the average

Overview

Boilermakers and boilermaker mechanics construct, assemble, and repair boilers, vats, tanks, and other large metal vessels that are designed to hold liquids and gases. Following blueprints, they lay out, cut, fit, bolt, weld, and rivet together heavy metal plates, boiler tubes, and castings. Boilermaker mechanics maintain and repair boilers and other vessels made by boilermakers. There are approximately 27,000 boilermakers working in the United States.

History

Boilers first became important during the Industrial Revolution, when steam power emerged as a practical way to drive various kinds of machinery. A boiler is an apparatus that heats a liquid, usually water, and converts it to vapor. Boilers were first made and used in England in the beginning of the 18th century. Manufacturers first used iron and then began using steel in boilers because steel could withstand more heat and pressure in use. During the 19th and 20th centuries, a series of design changes and improved alloys made boilers useful in a wide variety of industrial applications.

Because boilers are often operated at extremely high pressures, faulty construction, bad repairs, or improper operation can be very dangerous. During the late 19th century, regulations were put in place in some localities to prevent accidents caused by careless construction. Workers in the industry began organizing in the 1880s. By 1893, the two unions representing workers in boiler and similar trades met in Chicago to unite into what was then called the International Brotherhood of Boiler Makers, Iron Ship Builders, Blacksmiths, Forgers, and Helpers.

It was not until 1908, however, that rules and regulations were developed to apply to any sizable area. Massachusetts created a Board of Boiler Rules in that year, and Ohio followed with its own set of rules in 1911. By 1934, 19 states and 15 cities had such codes. Today, as a result of the combined efforts of industry, labor unions, and government, safety codes are practically universal. The American Society of Mechanical Engineers and the International Brotherhood of Boilermakers have been leaders in the promotion and enforcement of the codes of safe manufacture and maintenance.

The Job

Some boilermakers and mechanics work at or near the site where the boiler, tank, or vat is installed. Such sites include petroleum refineries, schools and other institutions with large heating plants, factories where boilers are used to generate power to run machines, factories that make and store products, such as chemicals or beer in large tanks, and atomic energy plants. Others work in shops or factories where boilers and other large vessels are manufactured.

Boilermakers who do layout work usually work in a shop or factory. These workers follow drawings, blueprints, and patterns to mark pieces of metal plate and tubing to indicate how the metal will be cut and shaped by other workers into the sections of vessels. Once the sections are fabricated, other workers at the shop, called fitters, temporarily put together the plates and the framework of the vessels. They check the drawings and other specifications and bolt or tack-weld pieces together to be sure that the parts fit properly.

In doing the final assembly at the site, boilermakers first refer to blueprints and mark off dimensions on the base that has been prepared for the finished vessel. They use measuring devices, straightedges, and transits. They attach rigging equipment, such as hoists, jacks, and rollers, to any prefabricated sections of the vessel that are so large they must be lifted into place with cranes. After crane operators move the sections to the correct positions, the boilermakers fine-tune the alignment of the parts. They use levels and check plumb lines and then secure the sections in place with wedges and turnbuckles. With cutting torches, files, and grinders, they remove irregularities and precisely adjust the fit and finally weld and rivet the sections together. They may also attach other tubing, valves, gauges, or other parts to the vessel and then test the container for leaks and defects.

Boilermakers also work in shipbuilding and in repairing the hulls, bulkheads, and decks of iron ships. In a typical repair, boilermakers first remove damaged metal plates by drilling out rivets and cutting off rivet heads with a chipping hammer. Then they take measurements of the damaged plates or make wooden patterns of them so that new plates can be made. They install the new plates, reaming and aligning rivet holes, then fastening on the plates by driving in rivets. Sometimes similar work is done on ships' boilers, condensers, evaporators, loaders, gratings, and stacks.

Field construction boilermakers work outdoors and move from one geographic location to another. They join construction teams in erecting and repairing pressure vessels, air pollution equipment, blast furnaces, water treatment plants, storage tanks, and stacks and liners. They can be involved in the erection of a 750,000-gallon water storage tank, the placement of a nuclear power plant reactor dome, or the construction of components on a hydroelectric power station.

Boilermaker mechanics maintain and repair boilers and other vessels. They routinely clean or direct others to clean boilers, and they inspect fittings, valves, tubes, controls, and other parts. When necessary, they check the vessels to identify specific weaknesses or sources of trouble. They update components, such as burners and boiler tubes, to make them as efficient as possible. They dismantle the units to replace worn or defective parts, using hand and power tools, gas torches, and welding equipment. Sometimes repairs require that they use metalworking machinery, such as power shears and presses, to cut and shape parts to specification. They strengthen joints and supports, and they put patches on weak areas of metal plates. Like fabrication and installation work, all repairs must be done in compliance with state and local safety codes.

Requirements

HIGH SCHOOL
A high school diploma is required for applicants to the boilermaking trade. In the past, people have become boilermakers through on-the-job training, but apprenticeships are now strongly recommended. To gain an apprenticeship, an applicant must score well on an aptitude test. You can prepare yourself for this test and the career by taking math classes and shop classes throughout high school. Courses that give you the opportunity to learn blueprint reading, welding, and metalworking are especially helpful.

POSTSECONDARY TRAINING
Formal apprenticeships usually last four years. An apprentice receives practical training while working as a helper under the supervision of an experienced boilermaker. In addition to working, trainees attend classes in the technical aspects of the trade. Apprentices study subjects such as blueprint reading, layout, welding techniques, mechanical drawing, the physics and chemistry of various metals, and applied mathematics. While on the job, apprentices practice the knowledge they have acquired in the classroom. They develop such skills as using rigging and hoisting equipment, welding, riveting, and installing auxiliary devices and tubes onto vessels.

OTHER REQUIREMENTS
Mechanical aptitude and manual dexterity are important characteristics for prospective boilermakers. Because the work can be very strenuous, stamina is needed for jobs that require a great deal of bending, stooping, squatting, or reaching. Before they begin work, boilermakers may need to pass a physical examination showing that they are in good enough health to do the work safely. On the job, they must be able to work well despite noisy surroundings, odors, working at heights or in small enclosed spaces, and other discomforts and dangers. It is also important that they be cautious and careful in their work and that they closely follow safety rules.

Exploring

You may be able to observe boilermakers or workers who use similar skills as they work on construction projects or repair and maintenance jobs. For example, welders and equipment operators lifting heavy objects with elaborate rigging can sometimes be seen working at sites where large buildings are being erected. High school shop courses, such as blueprint reading and metalworking, can give you an idea of some of the activities of boilermakers. With the help of shop teachers or guidance counselors, you may be able to arrange to talk with people working in the trade. Information may also be obtained by contacting the local union-management committee in charge of apprenticeships for boilermakers.

Employers

Approximately 27,000 boilermakers work in the United States. Of that number, slightly more than half work in the construction industry. Others work in manufacturing, employed primarily in boiler manufacturing shops, iron and steel plants, petroleum refineries, chemical plants, and shipyards. Still others work for boiler repair firms, for railroads, and in navy shipyards and federal power facilities.

Starting Out

There are a limited number of apprenticeships available in boilermaking; only the best applicants are accepted, and there may be a waiting period before the apprenticeship starts. Sometimes workers begin as helpers in repair shops and enter formal apprenticeships later. These helper jobs are often advertised in newspapers. Vocational and technical schools and sometimes high schools with metal shop courses may also help their graduates locate such positions. Other good approaches are to apply directly to employers and to contact the local office of the state employment service.

Advancement

Upon completing their training programs, apprentices qualify as journeymen boilermakers. With experience and the right kind of leadership abilities, boilermakers may be able to advance to supervisory positions. In fabrication shops, layout workers and fitters who start as helpers can learn the skills they need in about two years. In time, they may move up to become shop supervisors, or they may decide to become boilermakers who work on-site to assemble vessels.

Earnings

According to the U.S. Department of Labor, the median hourly wage for boilermakers in 2000 was $17.80. For full-time work at 40 hours per week, this wage translates into a median annual income of $37,024. The department also reported that the lowest-paid 10 percent earned less than $9.60 per hour, or less than approximately $19,970 per year for full-time work. At the other end of the pay scale, the highest-paid 10 percent made more than $26.81 per hour (approximately $55,765 annually).

According to the International Brotherhood of Boilermakers, annual earnings vary greatly because of the temporary, cyclical nature of the work. Apprentices start at about 60 percent of journeyman wages. Earnings also vary according to the part of the country where boilermakers work, the industry that employs them, and their level of skill and experience. Pay rates are usually highest for boilermakers doing installation work in the construction industry and lower for those in manufacturing industries, although workers in construction may not be employed as steadily. Workers in the Northeast, the Great Lakes area, and cities in the far West tend to earn the highest wages.

Boilermakers tend to make more than boilermaker mechanics. Among employees in boiler-fabrication shops, layout workers generally earn more, while fitters earn less. Both layout workers and fitters normally work indoors; therefore, their earnings are not limited by seasonal variations in weather.

Most boilermakers are members of unions, and union contracts set their wages and benefits. The largest union is the International Brotherhood of Boilermakers, Iron Ship Builders, Blacksmiths, Forgers, and Helpers. Other boilermakers are members of the Industrial Union of Marine and Shipbuilding Workers of America; the Oil, Chemical, and Atomic Workers International Union; the United Steelworkers of America; the International Association of Machinists and Aerospace Workers; and the United Automobile, Aerospace, and Agricultural Implement Workers of America. Among the fringe benefits established under union contracts are health insurance, pension plans, and paid vacation time.

Work Environment

Boilermaking tends to be more hazardous than many other occupations. Boilermakers often work with dangerous tools and equipment; they must manage heavy materials; and they may climb to heights to do installation or repair work. Despite great progress in preventing accidents, the rate of on-the-job injuries for boilermakers remains higher than the average for all manufacturing industries. Employer and union safety programs and standards set by the federal government's Occupational Safety and Health Administration are helping to control dangerous conditions and reduce accidents.

This work often requires physical exertion and may be carried on in extremely hot, poorly ventilated, noisy, and damp places. At times it is necessary to work in cramped quarters inside boilers, vats, or tanks. At other times, workers must handle materials and equipment several stories above ground level. Sometimes installation workers work on jobs that require them to remain away from home for considerable periods of time.

To protect against injury, boilermakers and mechanics use a variety of special clothing and equipment, such as hard hats, safety glasses and shoes, harnesses, and respirators. A 40-hour week is average, but in some jobs, deadlines may require overtime.

Outlook

The U.S. Department of Labor projects little or no change in the employment rate of boilermakers through 2010. One reason for this is the current trend of repairing and retrofitting, rather than replacing, boilers. In addition, the smaller boilers currently being used require less on-site assembly. Finally, the automation of production technologies and the increasing use of imported boilers will cut down on the need for boilermakers.

During economic downturns, boilermakers, including layout workers and fitters, may be laid off because many industries stop expanding their operations and install very few new boilers. On the other hand, boilermaker mechanics are less affected by downturns because they work more on maintaining and repairing existing equipment, which requires their services regardless of economic conditions.

Despite little projected growth, there will be openings for boilermakers every year as experienced workers leave the field. Workers who have completed apprenticeships will have the best opportunities for good jobs.

For More Information

For information about boilermaker apprenticeships, contact:
BOILERMAKERS NATIONAL APPRENTICESHIP PROGRAM
1017 North 9th Street
Kansas City, KS 66101
Tel: 913-342-2100
Email: info@bnap.com
Web: http://www.bnap.com

For additional career information, contact:
INTERNATIONAL BROTHERHOOD OF BOILERMAKERS, IRON SHIP BUILDERS, BLACKSMITHS, FORGERS AND HELPERS, AFL-CIO
753 State Avenue
Kansas City, KS 66102
Tel: 913-371-2640
Web: http://www.boilermakers.org

Communications Equipment Technicians

Quick Facts

School Subjects
  Mathematics
  Technical/shop
Personal Skills
  Following instructions
  Mechanical/manipulative
Work Environment
  Primarily indoors
  Primarily multiple locations
Minimum Education Level
  Some postsecondary training
Salary Range
  $19,530 to $44,030 to $56,640+
Certification or Licensing
  Required for certain positions
Outlook
  Decline

Overview

Communications equipment technicians install, test, maintain, troubleshoot, and repair a wide variety of telephone and radio equipment used to transmit communications—voices and data—across long distances. This does not include, however, equipment that handles entertainment broadcast to the public via radio or television signals. Most communications equipment technicians work in telephone company offices or on customers' premises. In the United States, approximately 196,000 people work as communications equipment technicians.

History

Alexander Graham Bell (1847-1922) patented the first practical telephone in 1876. By 1878, a commercial telephone company that switched calls between its local customers was operating in New Haven, Connecticut. For many years, telephone connections were made by operators who worked at central offices of telephone companies. A company customer who wanted to speak with another customer had to call the operator at a central office, and the operator would connect the two customer lines together by inserting a metal plug into a socket.

Today, automatic switching equipment has replaced operators for routine connections like this, and telephones are carrying much more than voice messages between local customers. Vast quantities of information are sent across phone lines in the form of visual images, computer data, and telegraph and teletypewriter signals. Furthermore, telephone systems today are part of larger interconnected telecommunications systems. These systems link together telephones with other equipment that sends information via microwave and television transmissions, fiber optics cables, undersea cables, and signals bounced off satellites in space. High-speed computerized switching and routing equipment makes it possible for telecommunications systems to handle millions of calls and other data signals at the same time.

The Job

Although specific duties vary, most communications equipment technicians share some basic kinds of activities. They work with electrical measuring and testing devices and hand tools; read blueprints, circuit diagrams, and electrical schematics (diagrams); and consult technical manuals. The following paragraphs describe just a few of the many technicians who work in this complex industry.

Central office equipment installers, also called *equipment installation technicians,* are specialists in setting up and taking down the switching and dialing equipment located in telephone company central offices. They install equipment in newly established offices, update existing equipment, add on to facilities that are being expanded, and remove old, outdated apparatus.

Central office repairers, also called *switching equipment technicians* or *central office technicians,* work on the switching equipment that automatically connects lines when customers dial calls. They analyze defects and malfunctions in equipment, make fine adjustments, and test and repair switches and relays. These workers use various special tools, gauges, and meters as well as ordinary hand tools.

PBX systems technicians or *switching equipment technicians* work on PBXs, or private branch exchanges, which are direct lines that businesses install to bypass phone company lines. PBX systems can handle both voice and data communications and can provide specialized services such as electronic mail and automatic routing of calls at the lowest possible cost.

PBX installers install these systems. They may assemble customized switchboards for customers. *PBX repairers* maintain and repair PBX systems and associated equipment. In addition, they may work on mobile radiophones and microwave transmission devices.

Maintenance administrators test customers' lines within the central office to find causes and locations of malfunctions reported by customers. They report the nature of the trouble to maintenance crews and coordinate their activities to clear up the trouble. Some maintenance administrators work in cable television company offices, diagnosing subscribers' problems with cable television signals and dispatching repairers if necessary. They use highly automated testboards and other equipment to analyze circuits. They enter data into computer files and interpret computer output about trouble areas in the system.

Many workers in this group are concerned with other kinds of communications equipment that are not part of telephone systems. Among these are *radio repairers and mechanics,* who install and repair radio transmitters and receivers. Sometimes they work on other electronics equipment at microwave and fiber optics installations. *Submarine cable equipment technicians* work on the machines and equipment used to send messages through underwater cables. Working in cable offices and stations, they check and adjust transmitters and printers and repair or replace faulty parts. *Office electricians* maintain submarine cable circuits and rearrange connections to ensure that cable service is not interrupted. *Avionics technicians* work on electronic components in aircraft communication, navigation, and flight control systems. *Signal maintainers* or *track switch maintainers* work on railroads. They install, inspect, and maintain the signals, track switches, gate crossings, and communications systems throughout rail networks. *Instrument repairers* work in repair shops, where they repair, test, and modify a variety of communications equipment.

Requirements

HIGH SCHOOL

Most employers prefer to hire candidates with at least some postsecondary training in electronics. So to prepare for this career, you should take computer courses, algebra, geometry, English, physics, and shop classes in high school. Useful shop courses are those that introduce you to principles of electricity and electronics, basic machine repair, reading blueprints and engineering drawings, and using hand tools.

POSTSECONDARY TRAINING

Most telecommunications employers prefer to hire technicians who have already learned most of the necessary skills, so consider getting training in this area either through service in the military or from a postsecondary training program. Programs at community or junior colleges or technical schools in telecommunications technology, electronics, electrical, or electromechanical technology, or even computer maintenance or related subjects, may be appropriate for people who want to become communications equipment technicians. Most programs last two years, although certification in specific areas often can be obtained through a one-year program. Useful classes are those that provide practical knowledge about electricity and electronics and teach the use of hand tools, electronic testing equipment, and computer data terminals. Classes in digital and fiber optic technology are also beneficial.

Applicants for entry-level positions may have to pass tests of their knowledge, general mechanical aptitude, and manual dexterity. Once hired, employees often go through company training programs. They may study practical and theoretical aspects of electricity, electronics, and mathematics that they will need to know for their work. Experienced workers also may attend training sessions from time to time. They need to keep their knowledge up to date, as new technology in the rapidly changing telecommunications field affects the way they do their jobs.

CERTIFICATION OR LICENSING

Some workers in this field must obtain a license. Federal Communications Commission regulations require that anyone who works with radio transmitting equipment must have a Global Maritime Distress and Safety System license. In order to receive a license, applicants need to pass a written test on radio laws and operating procedures and take a Morse code examination.

Certification for technicians is available from the National Association of Radio and Telecommunications Engineers. To receive certification, you'll need a certain amount of education and experience in telecommunications, and you'll have to pass an examination.

OTHER REQUIREMENTS

You'll need strong mechanical and electrical aptitudes as well as manual dexterity. Keep in mind, too, that you'll need to be able to distinguish between colors because many wires are color-coded. You should also have problem-solving abilities and the ability to work without a lot of direct supervision. Math and computer skills are very important; you'll also need to be able to interpret very technical manuals and blueprints. You'll be expected to keep accurate records, so you'll need to be organized.

Exploring

In high school, you can begin to find out about the work of communications equipment technicians by taking whatever electronics, computer, and electrical shop courses are available as well as other shop courses that help you become familiar with using various tools. Teachers or guidance counselors may be able to help you arrange a visit to a telephone company central office, where you can see telephone equipment and observe workers on the job. It may be possible to obtain a part-time or summer-helper job at a business that sells and repairs electronics equipment. Such a job could provide the opportunity to talk to workers whose skills are similar to those needed by many communications equipment technicians. Serving in the armed forces in a communications section can also provide a way to learn about this field and gain some useful experience.

Employers

Local and long-distance telephone companies and manufacturers of telephone and other electronic communications equipment employ communications equipment technicians. Work is also available with electrical repair shops and cable television companies.

Starting Out

Beginning technicians can apply directly to the employment office of the local telephone company. Many times it is necessary for newly hired workers to take a position in a different part of the company until an opening as a technician becomes available. However, telephone companies have been reducing the number of technicians they need in recent years, and competition for these positions is especially heavy.

Information on job openings in this field may be available through the offices of the state employment service and through classified advertisements in newspapers. Because many communications equipment technicians are members of unions such as the Communications Workers of America (CWA) and the International Brotherhood of Electrical Workers, job seekers can contact their local offices for job leads and assistance or visit the CWA Web site. The Personal Communications Industry Association also offers free job listings on its Wireless Jobnet online. Graduates of technical programs may be able to find out about openings at local companies through the school's job placement services or through contacts with teachers and administrators.

Advancement

The advancement possibilities for communications equipment technicians depend on the area of the telecommunications industry in which they work. Because of changes in equipment and technology, workers who hope to advance will need to have received recent training or update their skills through additional training. This training may be offered through employers or can be obtained through technical institutes or telecommunications associations.

Advancement opportunities in telephone companies may be limited because of the fact that many telephone companies are reducing their workforces and will have less need for certain types of workers in the future. This will result in fewer positions to move into and increased competition for more advanced positions. However, some workers may be able to advance to supervisory or administrative positions.

Many workers can advance through education resulting in an associate's or bachelor's degree. Workers who have completed two- or four-year programs in electrical or telecommunications engineering programs have the best opportunity to advance and can become engineering assistants, engineers, or telecommunications specialists.

Earnings

Earnings vary among communications equipment workers depending on their area of specialization, the size of their employer, and their location. The U.S. Department of Labor reports that median hourly earnings for telecommunications equipment installers and repairers were $21.17 in 2000. A technician earning this amount and working full-time at 40 hours a week would have a yearly income of approximately $44,030. The lowest-paid 10 percent of telecommunications equipment technicians earned less than $12.04 per hour (approximately $25,040 yearly); the highest-paid 10 percent earned more than $27.23 per hour (approximately $56,640 annually).

The Department of Labor also reports that the 2000 median hourly wage for radio mechanics was $15.86. The annual income for a technician working full-time at this pay rate would be approximately $32,990. At the low end of the pay scale, 10 percent made less than $9.39 hourly (approximately $19,530 per year); at the high end, 10 percent made more than $25.62 hourly (approximately $53,290 annually).

Most workers in this group who are employed by telephone companies are union members, and their earnings are set by contracts between the union and the company. Many currently employed communications equipment technicians have several years of experience and are at the higher end of the pay scale. Most workers in this field receive extra pay for hours worked at night, on weekends, or over 40 hours a week. Benefits vary but generally include paid vacations, paid holidays, sick leave, and health insurance. In addition, some companies offer pension and retirement plans.

Work Environment

Communications equipment technicians usually work 40 hours a week. Some work shifts at night, on weekends, and on holidays because telecommunications systems must give uninterrupted service, and trouble can occur at any time.

Central telephone offices are clean, well lighted, and well ventilated. Communications equipment technicians may also be working on site, which may require some crawling around on office floors and some bending. Even if these workers are running cables, they aren't likely to be doing much heavy lifting; machinery assists them in some of the more strenuous work. These workers may work alone, or they may be supervising the work of others. Some communications equipment technicians also work directly with clients.

The work can be stressful, as technicians are often expected to work quickly to remedy urgent problems with communications equipment. Some technicians who work for large companies with clients nationwide must also travel as part of their jobs.

Outlook

The U.S. Department of Labor predicts that the overall employment rate for communications equipment technicians will decline through 2010. Nevertheless, job availability will depend on the technician's area of specialization. For example, technicians working as central office and PBX installers should find numerous job opportunities, in part because growing use of the Internet places new demands on communications networks. On the other hand, employment for radio mechanics and other installers is expected to decline as pre-wired buildings and extremely reliable equipment translate into less need for maintenance and repair. New technology relies on transmission through telecommunications networks rather than central-office switching equipment. There are far fewer mechanical devices that break, wear out, and need to be periodically cleaned and lubricated. These networks contain self-diagnosing features that detect problems and, in some cases, route operations around a trouble spot until repairs can be made. When problems occur, it is usually easier to replace parts than to repair them. Competition for existing positions will be keen, and workers with the best qualifications stand the best chance of obtaining available jobs.

For More Information

To learn about issues affecting jobs in telecommunications, contact or visit the CWA Web site.
COMMUNICATIONS WORKERS OF AMERICA (CWA)
501 Third Street, NW
Washington, DC 20001-2797
Web: http://www.cwa-union.org

For information on union membership, contact:
INTERNATIONAL BROTHERHOOD OF ELECTRICAL WORKERS
1125 15th Street, NW
Washington, DC 20005
Web: http://ibew.org

For information on certification, contact:
NATIONAL ASSOCIATION OF RADIO AND TELECOMMUNICATIONS ENGINEERS
PO Box 678
167 Village Street
Medway, MA 02053
Tel: 800-896-2783
Web: http://www.narte.org

For information on educational programs and job opportunities in wireless technology (cellular, PCS, and satellite), contact:
PERSONAL COMMUNICATIONS INDUSTRY ASSOCIATION
500 Montgomery Street, Suite 700
Alexandria, VA 22314-1561
Tel: 800-759-0300
Web: http://www.pcia.com

For information about conferences, special programs, and membership, contact:
WOMEN IN CABLE AND TELECOMMUNICATIONS
230 West Monroe, Suite 2630
Chicago, IL 60606
Tel: 312-634-2330
Email: information@wict.org
Web: http://www.wict.org

Diesel Mechanics

Overview

Diesel mechanics repair and maintain diesel engines that power trucks, buses, ships, construction and roadbuilding equipment, farm equipment, and some automobiles. They may also maintain and repair nonengine components, such as brakes, electrical systems, and heating and air conditioning. There are approximately 285,000 diesel mechanics employed in the United States.

History

In 1892, Rudolf Diesel patented an engine that despite its weight and large size was more efficient than the gasoline engine patented by Gottlieb Daimler less than a decade earlier. While Daimler's engine became the standard for automobiles, Diesel found his engine had practical use for industry. The diesel engine differs from the gasoline engine in that the ignition of fuel is caused by compression of air in the engine's cylinders rather than by a spark. Diesel's engines were eventually used to power pipelines, electric and water plants, automobiles and trucks, and marine craft. Equipment used in mines, oil fields, factories and transoceanic shipping also came to rely on diesel engines. With the onset of World War I, diesel engines became standard in submarines, tanks, and other heavy equipment. Suddenly, diesel mechanics were in big demand, and the armed forces established training programs. Combat units supported by diesel-powered machines often had several men trained in diesel mechanics to repair breakdowns. The war proved to industry that diesel engines were tough and efficient, and many companies found applications for diesel-powered machines in the following years.

At the turn of the century, trucks were wooden wagons equipped with gasoline engines. As they became larger, transported more goods, and traveled farther, fuel efficiency became a big concern. In 1930, the trucking industry adopted the diesel engine, with its efficiency and durability, as its engine for the future. Many diesel mechanics began their training as automobile mechanics and learned diesel through hands-on experience. World War II brought a new demand for highly trained diesel mechanics, and again the armed forces trained men in diesel technology. After the war, diesel mechanics found new jobs in diesel at trucking companies that maintained large fleets of trucks and at construction companies that used diesel-powered equipment. It wasn't until the 1970s that diesel engines in consumer passenger cars began to gain popularity. Before then, the disadvantages of diesel—its heaviness, poor performance, and low driving comfort—made diesel a second choice for many consumers. But the fuel crisis of the 1970s brought diesel a greater share of the automotive market, creating more demand for mechanics who could repair and maintain diesel engines.

Today, job growth and security for diesel mechanics is closely tied to the trucking industry. In the 1980s and 1990s, the trucking industry experienced steady growth as other means of transportation, such as rail, were used less frequently. Now, many businesses and manufacturers have found it cost efficient to maintain less inventory. Instead, they prefer to have their materials shipped on an as-needed basis. This low-inventory system has created a tremendous demand on the trucking industry, and diesel mechanics are essential to helping the industry meet that demand.

The Job

Most diesel mechanics work on the engines of heavy trucks, such as those used in hauling freight over long distances, or in heavy industries such as construction and mining. Many are employed by companies that maintain their own fleet of vehicles. The diesel mechanic's main task is preventive maintenance to avoid breakdowns, but mechanics also make engine repairs when necessary. Diesel mechanics also frequently perform maintenance on other nonengine components, such as brake systems, electronics, transmissions, and suspensions.

Through periodic maintenance, diesel mechanics keep vehicles or engines in good operating condition. They run through a checklist of standard maintenance tasks, such as changing oil and filters, checking cooling systems, and inspecting brakes and wheel bearings for wear. They make the appropriate repairs or adjustments and replace parts that are worn. Fuel injection units, fuel pumps, pistons, crankshafts, bushings, and bearings must be regularly removed, reconditioned, or replaced.

As more diesel engines rely on a variety of electronic components, mechanics have become more proficient in the basics of electronics. Previously technical functions in diesel equipment (both engine and nonengine parts) are being replaced by electronics, significantly altering the way mechanics perform maintenance and repairs. As new technology evolves, diesel mechanics may need additional training to use tools and computers to diagnose and correct problems with electronic parts. Employers generally provide this training.

Diesel engines are scheduled for periodic rebuilding usually every 18 months or 100,000 miles. Mechanics rely upon extensive records they keep on each engine to determine the extent of the rebuild. Records detail the maintenance and repair history that helps mechanics determine repair needs and prevent future breakdowns. Diesel mechanics use various specialty instruments to make precision measurements and diagnostics of each engine component. Micrometers and various gauges test for engine wear. Ohmmeters, ammeters, and voltmeters test electrical components. Dynamometers and oscilloscopes test overall engine operations.

Engine rebuilds usually require several mechanics, each specializing in a particular area. They use ordinary hand tools such as ratchets and sockets, screwdrivers, wrenches, and pliers; power tools such as pneumatic wrenches; welding and flame-cutting equipment; and machine tools such as lathes and boring machines. Diesel mechanics supply their own hand tools at an investment of $6,000 to $25,000, depending on their specialty. It is the employer's responsibility to furnish the larger power tools, engine analyzers, and other diagnostic equipment.

In addition to trucks and buses, diesel mechanics also service and repair construction equipment such as cranes, bulldozers, earth-moving equipment, and road construction equipment. The variations in transmissions, gear systems, electronics, and other engine components of diesel engines may require additional training.

To maintain and increase their skills and to keep up with new technology, diesel mechanics must regularly read service and repair manuals, industry bulletins, and other publications. They must also be willing to take part in training programs given by manufacturers or at vocational schools. Those who have certification must periodically retake exams to keep their credentials. Frequent changes in technology demand that mechanics keep up to date with the latest training.

Requirements

HIGH SCHOOL
A high school diploma is the minimum requirement to land a job that offers growth possibilities, a good salary, and challenges. In addition to automotive and shop classes, high school students should take mathematics, English, and computer classes. Adjustments and repairs to many car components require the mechanic to make numerous computations, for which good mathematical skills will be essential. Diesel mechanics must be voracious readers in order to stay competitive; there are many must-read volumes of repair manuals and trade journals. Computer skills are also important, as computers are common in most repair shops.

POSTSECONDARY TRAINING
Employers prefer to hire those who have completed some kind of formal training program in diesel mechanics, or in some cases automobile mechanics—usually a minimum of two years' education in either case. A wide variety of such programs are offered at community colleges and vocational schools and by independent organizations and manufacturers. Most accredited programs include periods of internship.

Some programs are conducted in association with truck and heavy equipment manufacturers. Students combine work experience with hands-on classroom study of up-to-date equipment provided by manufacturers. In other programs, students alternate time in the classroom with internships at manufacturers. Although these students may take up to four years to finish their training, they become familiar with the latest technology and also earn modest salaries as they train.

CERTIFICATION OR LICENSING
One indicator of quality for entry-level mechanics recognized by everyone in the industry is certification by the National Institute for Automotive Service Excellence. Mechanics can become certified in one or more of several areas of heavy-duty truck repair or school bus repair.

To obtain certification, a candidate must pass one or more exams and show proof of two years of relevant work experience. Retesting is required every five years to maintain certification.

OTHER REQUIREMENTS

Diesel mechanics must be patient and thorough in their work. They need to have excellent troubleshooting skills and must be able to logically deduce the cause of system malfunctions. Diesel mechanics also need a Class A driver's license.

Exploring

Many community centers offer general auto maintenance workshops where students can get additional practice working on cars and learn from instructors. Trade magazines such as *Landline* (http://www.landlinemag.com) and *Overdrive* (http://www.overdriveonline.com) are an excellent source for learning what's new in the trucking industry and can be found at libraries and some larger bookstores. Working part-time at a repair shop or dealership can prepare students for the atmosphere and challenges a mechanic faces on the job.

Many diesel mechanics begin their exploration on gasoline engines because spare diesel engines are hard to come by for those who are just trying to learn and experiment. Diesel engines are very similar to gasoline engines except for their ignition systems and size. Besides being larger, diesel engines are distinguished by the absence of common gasoline engine components such as spark plugs, ignition wires, coils, and distributors. Diesel mechanics use the same hand tools as automobile mechanics, however, and in this way learning technical aptitude on automobiles will be important for the student who wishes to eventually learn to work on diesel engines.

Employers

Diesel mechanics may find employment in a number of different areas. Many work for dealers that sell semi trucks and other diesel-powered equipment. About 20 percent of the country's 285,000 diesel mechanics work for local and long-distance trucking companies. Other mechanics maintain the buses and trucks of public transit companies, schools, or governments. Diesel mechanics can find work all over the country, in both large and small cities. Job titles may range from *bus maintenance technician* to *hydraulic system technician, clutch rebuilder,* and *heavy duty maintenance mechanic.* A small number of diesel mechanics may find jobs in the railway and industrial sectors and in marine maintenance.

Starting Out

The best way to begin a career as a diesel mechanic is to enroll in a post-secondary training program and obtain accreditation. Trade and technical schools nearly always provide job placement assistance for their graduates. Such schools usually have contacts with local employers who need to hire well-trained people. Often, employers post job openings at accredited trade schools in their area.

Although postsecondary training programs are more widely available and popular today, some mechanics still learn the trade on the job as apprentices. Their training consists of working for several years under the guidance of experienced mechanics. Trainees usually begin as helpers, lubrication workers, or service station attendants, and they gradually acquire the skills and knowledge necessary for many service or repair tasks. However, fewer employers today are willing to hire apprentices because of the time and cost it takes to train them. Those who do learn their skills on the job inevitably require some formal training if they wish to advance and stay in step with the changing industry.

Intern programs sponsored by truck manufacturers or independent organizations provide students with opportunities to actually work with prospective employers. Internships can provide students with valuable contacts who will be able to recommend future employers once students have completed their classroom training. Many students may even be hired by the company for which they interned.

Advancement

Typically the first step a mechanic must take to advance is to receive certification. There are six areas of certification available in heavy-duty truck repair: gasoline engines, diesel engines, drive train, brakes, suspension and steering, and electrical systems. There are seven areas of certification available in school bus repair: body systems and special equipment, diesel engines, drive train, brakes, suspension and steering, electrical/electronic systems, and air-conditioning systems and controls.

Although certification is voluntary, it is a widely recognized standard of achievement for diesel mechanics and the way many advance. The more certification a mechanic has, the more he or she is worth to an employer, and the higher he or she advances. Those who pass all seven exams earn the status of master truck mechanic. To maintain their certification, mechanics must retake the examination for their specialties every five years.

With today's complex diesel engine and truck components requiring hundreds of hours of study and practice to master, more employers prefer to hire certified mechanics. Certification assures the employer that the employee is skilled in the latest repair procedures and is familiar with the most current diesel technology. Those with good communication and planning skills may advance to shop supervisor or service manager at larger repair shops or companies that keep large fleets. Others with good business skills go into business for themselves and open their own shops or work as freelance mechanics. Some master mechanics may teach at technical and vocational schools or at community colleges.

Earnings

Diesel mechanics' earnings vary depending on their region, industry (trucking, construction, railroad), and other factors. Technicians in the West and Midwest tend to earn more than those in other regions, although these distinctions are gradually disappearing.

According to the U.S. Department of Labor, the median hourly pay for all diesel mechanics in 2000 was $15.55, or approximately $32,344 annually for full-time employment. The department also reported that the lowest-paid 10 percent of diesel mechanics earned approximately $9.88 an hour, while the highest-paid 10 percent earned more than $22.63 an hour. Mechanics who work for companies that must operate around the clock, such as bus lines, may work at night, on weekends, or on holidays and receive extra pay for this work. Some industries are subject to seasonal variations in employment levels, such as construction.

Among mechanics who service company vehicles, the best paid are usually those employed in the transportation industry. Diesel mechanics employed by companies in the manufacturing, wholesale, and retail trades and service industries have average hourly earnings that may be as much as 10 percent lower than transportation diesel mechanics.

Mechanics working for construction companies during peak summer building seasons earn up to $1,000 a week.

Many diesel mechanics are members of labor unions, and their wage rates are established by contracts between the union and the employer. Benefits packages vary from business to business. Mechanics can expect health insurance and paid vacation from most employers. Other benefits may include dental and eye care, life and disability insurance, and a pension plan. Employers usually cover a mechanic's work clothes through a clothing allowance and may pay a percentage of hand tool purchases. An increasing number of employers pay all or most of an employee's certification training if he or she passes the test. A mechanic's salary can increase by yearly bonuses or profit sharing if the business does well.

Work Environment

Depending on the size of the shop and whether it's a trucking or construction company, government, or private business, diesel mechanics work with anywhere from two to 20 other mechanics. Most shops are well lighted and well ventilated. They can be frequently noisy due to running trucks and equipment. Hoses are attached to exhaust pipes and led outside to avoid carbon monoxide poisoning.

Minor hand and back injuries are the most common problem for diesel mechanics. When reaching in hard-to-get-at places or loosening tight bolts, mechanics often bruise, cut, or burn their hands. With caution and experience, most mechanics learn to avoid hand injuries. Working for long periods of time in cramped or bent positions often results in a stiff back or neck. Diesel mechanics also lift many heavy objects that can cause injury if not handled cautiously; however, most shops have small cranes or hoists to lift the heaviest objects. Some may experience allergic reactions to the variety of solvents and oils frequently used in cleaning, maintenance, and repair. Shops must comply with strict safety procedures to help employees avoid accidents. Most mechanics work between 40- and 50-hour weeks, but they may be required to work longer hours when the shop is busy or during emergencies. Some mechanics make emergency repairs to stranded, roadside trucks or to construction equipment.

Outlook

With diesel technology getting better (smaller, smarter, and less noisy), more light trucks and other vehicles and equipment are switching to diesel engines. Diesel engines are already more fuel efficient than gasoline engines. Also, the increased reliance by businesses on quick deliveries has increased the demand on trucking companies. Many businesses maintain lower inventories of materials, instead preferring to have items shipped more frequently. The increase in diesel-powered vehicles, together with a trend toward increased cargo transportation via trucks, will create jobs for highly skilled diesel mechanics. Less-skilled workers will face tough competition. The U.S. Department of Labor predicts employment growth to be about as fast as the average through 2010.

Diesel mechanics enjoy good job security. Fluctuations in the economy have little effect on employment in this field. When the economy is bad, people service and repair their trucks and equipment rather than replace them. Conversely, when the economy is good, more people are apt to service their trucks and equipment regularly as well as buy new trucks and equipment.

The most jobs for diesel mechanics will open up at trucking companies that hire mechanics to maintain and repair their fleets. Construction companies are also expected to require an increase in diesel mechanics to maintain their heavy machinery, such as cranes, earthmovers, and other diesel-powered equipment.

For More Information

For information on the automotive service industry and continuing education programs, contact:
AUTOMOTIVE AFTERMARKET INDUSTRY ASSOCIATION
4600 East-West Highway, Suite 300
Bethesda, MD 20814-3415
Tel: 301-654-6664
Email: aaia@aftermarket.org
Web: http://www.aftermarket.org

For information on training, accreditation, and testing, contact:
INTER-INDUSTRY CONFERENCE ON AUTO COLLISION REPAIR
3701 Algonquin Road, Suite 400
Rolling Meadows, IL 60008
Tel: 800-422-7872
Web: http://www.i-car.com

For career information and information on certified programs, contact:
NATIONAL AUTOMOTIVE TECHNICIANS EDUCATION FOUNDATION
101 Blue Seal Drive, Suite 101
Leesburg, VA 20175
Tel: 703-669-6650
Web: http://www.natef.org

For information on becoming a certified mechanic, contact:
NATIONAL INSTITUTE FOR AUTOMOTIVE SERVICE EXCELLENCE
101 Blue Seal Drive, Suite 101
Leesburg, VA 20175
Tel: 877-ASE-TECH
Web: http://www.asecert.org

Elevator Installers and Repairers

Overview

Elevator installers and repairers, also called *elevator constructors* or *elevator mechanics,* are skilled crafts workers who assemble, install, and repair elevators, escalators, dumbwaiters, and similar equipment. They may also modernize this equipment when possible. Approximately 23,000 elevator installers and repairers are employed in the United States.

History

The use of mechanical devices for lifting loads dates back at least to the time of the ancient Romans, who used platforms attached to pulleys in constructing buildings. In the 17th century, a crude passenger elevator known as the "flying chair" was invented. These early elevators were operated by human, animal, or water power.

By the early 19th century, steam was used to power machines that raised elevators. For about the first half of the century, elevators were almost always used for lifting freight. This was because the hemp ropes that hauled the elevators were not strong enough to be safe for passenger use. In 1852, Elisha G. Otis designed and installed the first elevator with a safety device that prevented it from falling if the rope broke. Five years later, Otis's first safety elevator for carrying passengers was put into use in a store in New York City, and it was immediately declared a success.

Quick Facts

School Subjects
  Mathematics
  Technical/shop
Personal Skills
  Following instructions
  Mechanical/manipulative
Work Environment
  Primarily indoors
  Primarily multiple locations
Minimum Education Level
  Apprenticeship
Salary Range
  $23,275 to $47,382 to $69,118+
Certification or Licensing
  Required by certain states
Outlook
  About as fast as the average

Steam-powered elevators were used until the 1880s, when elevators powered by electricity were introduced. Subsequent design changes brought a series of improvements such as push-button operation, taller shafts, and faster speeds, so that the elevators could be used even in skyscrapers, and power doors and automatic operation, which made elevators more economical than they had been when human operators were necessary. Today's elevators often are controlled electronically and may be capable of moving up and down at 2,000 feet per minute.

The escalator, or moving stairway, was invented in 1891 by Jesse W. Reno. Early escalators, like modern ones, were electrically powered and resembled an inclined endless belt held in position by two tracks. Moving sidewalks and ramps are based on the same principle.

Almost as long as these machines have been in use in buildings to move people and their belongings, there has been a need for workers who specialize in assembling, installing, and maintaining them.

The Job

Elevator installers and repairers may service and update old equipment that has been in operation for many years, or they may work on new systems, which may be equipped with state-of-the-art microprocessors capable of monitoring a whole elevator system and automatically operating it with maximum possible efficiency. Installing and repairing modern elevators requires a good understanding of electricity, electronics, and hydraulics.

Installers begin their work by examining plans and blueprints that describe the equipment to be installed. They need to determine the layout of the components, including the framework, guide rails, motors, pumps, cylinders, plunger foundations, and electrical connections. Once the layout is clear, they install the guide rails (for guiding the elevator as it moves up and down) on the walls of the shaft. Then they run electrical wiring in the shaft between floors and install controls and other devices on each floor and at a central control panel. They assemble the parts of the car at the bottom of the shaft. They bolt or weld together the steel frame and attach walls, doors, and parts that keep the car from moving from side to side as it travels up and down the shaft. They also install the entrance doors and door frames on each floor.

Installers set up and connect the equipment that moves the cars. In cable elevator systems, steel cables are attached to each car and, at their other end, to a large counterweight. Hoisting machinery, often located at the top of the shaft, moves the cables around a pulley, thus moving the elevator car up or down and the counterweight in the opposite direction. In hydraulic systems, the car rests on a hydraulic cylinder that is raised and lowered by a pump, thus moving the elevator car up and down like an automobile on a lift. New technology also is becoming available to run elevators without cables, using magnetic fields instead. Regardless of the format, after the various parts of the elevator system are in place, the elevator installers test the operation of the system and make any necessary adjustments so that the installation meets building and safety code requirements.

In hotels, restaurants, hospitals, and other institutions where food is prepared, elevator installers may work on dumbwaiters, which are small elevators for transporting food and dishes from one part of a building to another. They may also work on escalators, installing wiring, motors, controls, the stairs, the framework for the stairs, and the tracks that keep the stairs in position. Increasingly, installers are working on APMs, or automated people-movers, the sort of "moving sidewalks" you might see at an airport.

After elevator and escalator equipment is installed, it needs regular adjustment and maintenance services to ensure that the system continues to function in a safe, reliable manner. Elevator repairers routinely inspect the equipment, perform safety tests using meters and gauges, clean parts that are prone to getting dirty, make adjustments, replace worn components, and lubricate bearings and other moving parts.

Repairers also do minor emergency repairs, such as replacing defective parts. Finding the cause of malfunctions often involves troubleshooting. For this reason, repairers need a strong mechanical aptitude. In addition, repairers may work as part of crews that do major repair and modernization work on older equipment.

Elevator installers and repairers use a variety of hand tools, power tools, welding equipment, and electrical testing devices such as digital multimeters, logic probes, and oscilloscopes.

Requirements

HIGH SCHOOL
Employers prefer to hire high school graduates who are at least 18 years of age and in good physical condition. Mechanical aptitude, an interest in machines, and some technical training related to the field are other

important qualifications. While you are in high school, therefore, take such classes as machine shop, electronics, and blueprint reading. Mathematics classes will teach you a variety of ways to work with numbers, and applied physics courses will give you a basis for understanding the workings of this equipment. Also, take English classes to enhance your verbal and writing skills. In this work you will be interacting with a variety of people, and communication skills will be a necessity.

POSTSECONDARY TRAINING

Union elevator installers and repairers receive their training through the National Elevator Industry (NEI) Educational Program, administered on a local level by committees made up of local employers who belong to the National Elevator Industry, Inc., and local branches of the International Union of Elevator Constructors. The programs consist of on-the-job training under the supervision of experienced workers, together with classroom instruction in related subjects. In the work portion of the program, trainees begin by doing the simplest tasks and gradually progress to more difficult activities. In the classroom, they learn about installation procedures, basic electrical theory, electronics, and job safety.

Union trainees spend their first six months in the industry in a probationary status. Those who complete the period successfully go on to become elevator constructor helpers. After an additional four to five years of required field and classroom education, they become eligible to take a validated mechanic exam. Upon passing this exam, workers become fully qualified journeymen installers and repairers. They may be able to advance more quickly if they already have a good technical background, acquired by taking courses at a postsecondary technical school or junior college.

CERTIFICATION OR LICENSING

Certification through the NEI Educational Program's training curriculum is required of new workers in this field. While union membership is not necessarily a requirement for employment, most elevator installers and repairers are members of the International Union of Elevator Constructors. Additionally, most states and municipalities require that elevator installers and repairers pass a licensing examination. This is not true of all areas at this time, but the trend is growing toward mandatory licensure.

OTHER REQUIREMENTS

Elevator installers and repairers must be in good physical shape because this job will require them to periodically carry heavy equipment or tools and work in small areas or in awkward positions. Elevator installers and repairers should also enjoy learning. To be successful in this field, they must constantly update their knowledge regarding new technologies, and continuing education through seminars, workshops, or correspondence courses is a must. Elevator installers and repairers need good hand-eye coordination. These workers should not be afraid of heights or of being in confined areas, since some of their work may take place in elevator shafts. Also, because elevator installers and repairers frequently work with electrical wiring and wires are typically color-coded based on their function, these workers need to have accurate color vision.

Exploring

High school courses such as electrical shop, machine shop, and blueprint reading can give you a hands-on sense of tasks that are similar to everyday activities of elevator installers and repairers. A part-time or summer job as a helper at a commercial building site may provide you with the opportunity to observe the conditions that these workers encounter on the job. If you or your guidance counselor can arrange for a tour of an elevator manufacturing firm, this experience will allow you to see how the equipment is built. One of the best ways to learn about the work may be to talk to a professional recommended by local representatives of the International Union of Elevator Constructors. You can ask this person about his or her training, what an average day on the job is like, what qualities he or she thinks a good elevator installer and repairer should have, and other questions that interest you.

Employers

The majority of elevator installers and repairers are employed by contractors specializing in work with elevators. Other elevator installers and repairers work for one of the more than 60 large elevator manufacturers such as Otis or Dover, for government agencies, or for small, local elevator maintenance contractors. Some larger institutions (such as hospitals, which run 24 hours a day) employ their own elevator maintenance and repair crews.

Starting Out

If you are seeking information about trainee positions in this field, you can contact the National Elevator Industry Educational Program or the International Union of Elevator Constructors for brochures. The local office of your state's employment service may also be a source of information and job leads.

Advancement

When an installer/repairer has completed the approximately five-year training program, met any local licensure requirements, and successfully passed a validated mechanic's exam, he or she is considered fully qualified—a journeyman. After gaining further experience, installers and repairers who work for elevator contracting firms may be promoted to positions such as *mechanic-in-charge* or *supervisor,* coordinating the work done by other installers. Other advanced positions include *adjusters,* highly skilled professionals who check equipment after installation and fine-tune it to specifications, and *estimators,* who figure the costs for supplies and labor for work before it is done. Those who work for an elevator manufacturer may move into sales positions, jobs related to product design, or management. Other experienced workers become *inspectors* employed by the government to inspect elevators and escalators to make sure that they comply with specifications and safety codes.

Earnings

Earnings depend on a variety of factors, such as experience and geographic location. Workers who are not fully qualified journeymen earn less than full-time professionals; for example, probationary workers start at about 50 percent of the full wage, and trainees earn about 70 percent of full wage. According to the U.S. Department of Labor, the median hourly wage for fully qualified elevator installers and repairers was $22.78 in 2001. This hourly wage translates into a yearly income of approximately $47,382 for full-time work. The department also reported that the lowest-paid 10 percent of installers and repairers made about $11.19 per hour (approximately $23,275 annually), while the highest-paid 10 percent earned more than $33.23 per hour (approximately $69,118 annually). In addition to regular wages, union elevator installers and repairers receive other benefits, including health insurance, pension plans, paid holidays and vacations, and some tuition-free courses in subjects related to their work. A recent change in the union contract called for the institution of a 40I-K retirement program.

Work Environment

The standard workweek for elevator installers and repairers is 40 hours. Some workers put in overtime hours (for which they are paid extra), and some repairers are on call for 24-hour periods to respond to emergency situations. Most repair work is done indoors, so little time is lost because of bad weather. It frequently is necessary to lift heavy equipment and parts and to work in very hot or cold, cramped, or awkward places.

Outlook

The U.S. Department of Labor predicts employment growth for elevator installers and repairers to be about as fast as the average through 2010, although a number of factors will influence this growth rate. Few new jobs are expected because this occupation employs so few workers. There will also be little need for replacement workers—the turnover in this field is relatively low because the extensive training people go through to gain these jobs results in high wages, which, in turn, result in workers remaining in the field. In addition, job outlook is somewhat dependent on the construction industry, particularly for new workers. Because installation of elevators is part of the interior work in new buildings, elevator installers are employed to work on sites about a year after construction begins. So, job availability in this field lags behind boom periods in the construction industry by about a year. Slowdowns in the building industry will eventually catch up to elevator installers, again lagging by about a year as installers complete previously assigned jobs.

Changes in the union contract that increased the retirement age for elevator installers and repairers brought many older workers back into the workforce in 1998. The NEI Educational Program expects new openings will become available in future years as these older workers retire. In addition, as the technology in the industry becomes more complex, employers will increasingly seek workers who are technically well trained.

For More Information

For information on benefits, scholarships, and job opportunities, contact:
INTERNATIONAL UNION OF ELEVATOR CONSTRUCTORS
5565 Sterret Place, Suite 310
Columbia, MD 21044
Tel: 410-997-9000
Email: info@iuec.org
Web: http://www.iuec.org

For industry news and information on continuing education, contact:
NATIONAL ASSOCIATION OF ELEVATOR CONTRACTORS
1298 Wellbrook Circle, Suite A
Conyers, GA 30012
Tel: 800-900-6232
Email: info@naec.org
Web: http://www.naec.org

For education, scholarship, and career information aimed at women in the construction industry, contact:
NATIONAL ASSOCIATION OF WOMEN IN CONSTRUCTION
327 South Adams Street
Fort Worth, TX 76104
Tel: 817-877-5551
Email: nawic@nawic.org
Web: http://www.nawic.org

For information on training in the elevator industry, contact:
NATIONAL ELEVATOR INDUSTRY EDUCATIONAL PROGRAM
11 Larsen Way
Attleboro Falls, MA 02763-1068
Tel. 508-699-2200
Web: http://www.neiep.org

Farm Equipment Mechanics

Overview

Farm equipment mechanics maintain, adjust, repair, and overhaul equipment and vehicles used in planting, cultivating, harvesting, moving, processing, and storing plant and animal farm products. Among the specialized machines with which they work are tractors, harvesters, combines, pumps, tilling equipment, silo fillers, hay balers, and sprinkler irrigation systems. They work for farm equipment repair shops, for farm equipment dealerships, and on large farms that have their own shops. There are approximately 41,000 farm equipment mechanics employed in the United States.

Quick Facts

School Subjects
  Agriculture
  Technical/shop
Personal Skills
  Mechanical/manipulative
  Technical/scientific
Work Environment
  Indoors and outdoors
  Primarily multiple locations
Minimum Education Level
  Some postsecondary training
Salary Range
  $16,952 to $25,750 to $37,918+
Certification or Licensing
  None available
Outlook
  Little change or more slowly
  than the average

History

The purpose of the mechanical devices used in farming has always been to increase production and decrease the need for human labor. In prehistoric times, people used simple wood and stone implements to help turn soil, plant seeds, and harvest crops more efficiently than they could with their bare hands. With the introduction of metal tools and the domestication of animals that could pull plows and vehicles, people were able to produce much more. Until the 19th century, farmers around the globe relied on human labor, animal power, and relatively simple equipment to accomplish all the tasks involved in agriculture.

Modern mechanized agriculture was developed in the 1800s. Initially, steam power was used for farm equipment. In the early part of the 20th century, gasoline-powered engines appeared. Shortly after, diesel engines were introduced to power various kinds of farm machinery. The use of motor-driven machines on farms had far-reaching effects. Machines improved agricultural productivity while lessening the need for human labor. As a result of increased use of farm machinery, the number of people working on farms has steadily decreased in many countries of the world.

In recent decades, farm machines have become large and complex, using electronic, computerized, and hydraulic systems. Agriculture is now a business operation that requires extremely expensive equipment capable of doing specialized tasks quickly and efficiently. Farmers cannot afford for their equipment to break down. They are now almost completely reliant on the dealers who sell them their equipment to be their source for the emergency repairs and routine maintenance services that keep the machines functioning well. Farm equipment mechanics are the skilled specialists who carry out these tasks, usually as employees of equipment dealers or of independent repair shops.

The Job

The success of today's large-scale farming operations depends on the reliability of many complex machines. It is the farm equipment mechanic's responsibility to keep the machines in good working order and repair or to overhaul them when they break down.

When farm equipment is not working properly, mechanics begin by diagnosing the problem. Using intricate testing devices, they are able to identify what is wrong. A compression tester, for example, can determine whether cylinder valves leak or piston rings are worn, and a dynamometer can measure engine performance. The mechanic will also examine the machine, observing and listening to it in operation and looking for clues such as leaks, loose parts, and irregular steering, braking, and gear shifting. It may be necessary to dismantle whole systems in the machine to diagnose and correct malfunctions.

When the problem is located, the broken, worn-out, or faulty components are repaired or replaced, depending on the extent of their defect. The machine or piece of equipment is reassembled, adjusted, lubricated, and tested to be sure it is again operating at its full capacity.

Farm equipment mechanics use many tools in their work. Besides hand tools such as wrenches, pliers, and screwdrivers and precision instruments such as micrometers and torque wrenches, they may use welding equipment, power grinders and saws, and other power tools. In addition, they do major repairs using machine tools such as drill presses, lathes, and milling and woodworking machines.

As farm equipment becomes more complex, mechanics are increasingly expected to have strong backgrounds in electronics. For instance, newer tractors have large, electronically controlled engines and air-conditioned cabs, as well as transmissions with many speeds.

Much of the time, farmers can bring their equipment into a shop, where mechanics have all the necessary tools available. But during planting or harvesting seasons, when timing may be critical for the farmers, mechanics are expected to travel to farms for emergency repairs in order to get the equipment up and running with little delay.

Farmers usually bring movable equipment into a repair shop on a regular basis for preventive maintenance services such as adjusting and cleaning parts and tuning engines. Routine servicing not only ensures fewer emergency repairs for the mechanics, but it also assures farmers that the equipment will be ready when it is needed. Shops in the rural outskirts of metropolitan areas often handle maintenance and repairs on a variety of lawn and garden equipment, especially lawn mowers.

If a mechanic works in a large shop, he or she may specialize in specific types of repairs. For example, a mechanic may overhaul gasoline or diesel engines, repair clutches and transmissions, or concentrate on the air-conditioning units in the cabs of combines and large tractors. Some mechanics, called *farm machinery set-up mechanics,* uncrate, assemble, adjust, and often deliver machinery to farm locations. Mechanics also do body work on tractors and other machines, repairing damaged sheet-metal body parts.

Some mechanics may work exclusively on certain types of equipment, such as hay balers or harvesters. Other mechanics work on equipment that is installed on the farms. For example, *sprinkler-irrigation equipment mechanics* install and maintain self-propelled circle-irrigation systems, which are like giant motorized lawn sprinklers. *Dairy equipment repairers* inspect and repair dairy machinery and equipment such as milking machines, cream separators, and churns.

Most farm equipment mechanics work in the service departments of equipment dealerships. Others are employed by independent repair shops. A smaller number work on large farms that have their own shops.

Requirements

HIGH SCHOOL
Take technical/shop courses that will introduce you to machinery repair, electrical work, and welding. Mechanical drawing classes can also prepare you for the work. Computer courses will be valuable; computers are used increasingly in farm machinery as well as in the administrative office of a machine repair and sales business. Science courses that include units in soil and agronomy will help you to understand the needs of the agriculture industry. As a member of the National FFA Organization (formerly the Future Farmers of America), you may be involved in special projects that include working with farm machinery.

POSTSECONDARY TRAINING
After graduating from high school, most farm equipment mechanics go on to complete a one- or two-year program in agricultural or farm mechanics at a vocational school or community college. If you can't find such a program, study in diesel mechanics or appropriate experience through the military are also options. Topics that you will learn about include the maintenance and repair of diesel and gasoline engines, hydraulic systems, welding, and electronics. Your education doesn't stop there, however. After completing one of these programs you will be hired as a trainee or helper and continue to learn on the job, receiving training from experienced mechanics.

Some farm equipment mechanics learn their trade through apprenticeship programs. These programs combine three to four years of on-the-job training with classroom study related to farm equipment repair and maintenance. Apprentices are usually chosen from among shop helpers.

To stay up to date on technological changes that affect their work, mechanics and trainees may take special short-term courses conducted by equipment manufacturers. In these programs, which usually last a few days, company service representatives explain the design and function of new models of equipment and teach mechanics how to maintain and repair them. Some employers help broaden their mechanics' skills by sending them to local vocational schools for special intensive courses in subjects such as air-conditioning repair, hydraulics, or electronics.

OTHER REQUIREMENTS

Farm machinery is usually large and heavy. Mechanics need the strength to lift heavy machine parts such as transmissions. They also need manual dexterity to be able to handle tools and small components. Farm equipment mechanics are usually expected to supply their own hand tools. After years of accumulating favorite tools, experienced mechanics may have collections that represent an investment of thousands of dollars. Employers generally provide all the large power tools and test equipment needed in the shop.

Exploring

Many people who go into farm equipment work have grown up with mechanical repair—they've experimented with lawn mowers, old cars, and other machinery, and they've used a lot of farm equipment. If you don't live on a farm, you may be able to find part-time or summer work on a farm. You can also get valuable mechanical experience working with a gasoline service station, automobile repair shop, or automotive supply house. Attending farm shows is a good way to learn about farm equipment and manufacturers. At shows, you may have the opportunity to talk to equipment manufacturers' representatives and learn more about new developments in the industry. In addition, consider joining a chapter of the National FFA Organization. This organization is open to students ages 12 to 21 who are enrolled in agricultural programs and offers a wide variety of activities, including career development programs.

Employers

Farm equipment mechanics work in all parts of the country, but there are more job opportunities in the "farm belt"—the Midwestern states. Work is available with independent repair and service businesses, large farm equipment sales companies, and large independent and commercial farms. Some mechanics are self-employed, running their own repair businesses in rural areas. Most independent repair shops employ fewer than five mechanics, while in dealers' service departments there may be 10 or more mechanics on the payroll.

Starting Out

Many people who become trainees in this field have prior experience in related occupations. They may have worked as farmers, farm laborers, heavy-equipment mechanics, automobile mechanics, or air-conditioning mechanics. Although people with this kind of related experience are likely to begin as helpers, their training period may be considerably shorter than the training for beginners with no such experience.

When looking for work, you should apply directly to local farm equipment dealers or independent repair shops. Graduates of vocational schools can often get help finding jobs through their schools' placement services. State employment service offices are another source of job leads as well as information on any apprenticeships that are available in the region.

Advancement

After they have gained some experience, farm equipment mechanics employed by equipment dealers may be promoted to such positions as shop supervisor, service manager, and eventually manager of the dealership. Some mechanics eventually decide to open their own repair shops (approximately 4 percent of all mechanics are self-employed). Others become service representatives for farm equipment manufacturers. Additional formal education, such as completion of a two-year associate's degree program in agricultural mechanics or a related field, may be required of service representatives.

Earnings

The U.S. Department of Labor reports farm equipment mechanics had median hourly earnings of $12.38 in 2000. This figure translates into a yearly income of approximately $25,750. In addition, the department reports that the lowest-paid farm equipment mechanics earned about $8.15 per hour ($16,952 per year), while the highest-paid earned $18.23 or more per hour ($37,918 or more per year). Exact earnings figures are difficult to determine because farm equipment mechanics do not generally work consistent 40-hour weeks throughout the year. During the busy planting and harvest seasons, for example, mechanics may work many hours of overtime, for which they are usually paid time-and-a-half rates.

This overtime pay can substantially increase their weekly earnings. However, during the winter months some mechanics may work less or they may be temporarily laid off, reducing their total income.

Employee benefits may be rare when working for a small shop. A large commercial farm or sales company may offer health insurance plans and sick leave.

Work Environment

Farm equipment mechanics generally work indoors on equipment that has been brought into the shop. Most modern shops are properly ventilated, heated, and lighted. Some older shops may be less comfortable. During harvest seasons, mechanics may have to leave the shop frequently and travel many miles to farms, where they perform emergency repairs outdoors in any kind of weather. They may often work six to seven days a week, 10 to 12 hours a day during this busy season. In the event of an emergency repair, a mechanic often works independently, with little supervision. Mechanics need to be self-reliant and able to solve problems under pressure. When a farm machine breaks down, the lost time can be very expensive for the farmer. A mechanic must be able to diagnose problems quickly and perform repairs without delay.

Grease, gasoline, rust, and dirt are part of the farm equipment mechanic's life. Although safety precautions have improved in recent years, mechanics are often at risk of injury when lifting heavy equipment and parts with jacks or hoists. Other hazards they must routinely guard against include burns from hot engines, cuts from sharp pieces of metal, and exposure to toxic farm chemicals. Following good safety practices can reduce the risk of injury to a minimum.

Outlook

The U.S. Department of Labor reports that employment of farm equipment mechanics will grow more slowly than the average for all occupations through 2010 because of the efficiency and dependability of modern farm equipment. To be competitive in the job market, a farm equipment mechanic may need a few years of college training along with some practical experience.

Advancements in technology have revolutionized farm equipment Those working with farm equipment will have to have an understanding

of computers, electronics, and highly sophisticated devices and, therefore, they will need more specialized training.

For More Information

For AEM press releases, equipment sales statistics, agricultural
reports, and other news of interest to farm mechanics, contact:
ASSOCIATION OF EQUIPMENT MANUFACTURERS (AEM)
10 South Riverside Plaza
Chicago, IL 60606-3710
Tel: 312-321-1470
Email: info@aem.org
Web: http://www.aem.org

At the FEMA Web site, you can learn about its publications, read
industry news, and find out about upcoming farm shows.
FARM EQUIPMENT MANUFACTURERS ASSOCIATION (FEMA)
1000 Executive Parkway, Suite 100
St. Louis, MO 63141-6369
Tel: 314-878-2304
Email: info@farmequip.org
Web: http://www.farmequip.org

For information on student chapters and the many activities available,
contact:
NATIONAL FFA ORGANIZATION
PO Box 68960
6060 FFA Drive
Indianapolis, IN 46268-0960
Tel: 317-802-6060
Web: http://www.ffa.org

Fluid Power
Technicians

Overview

Fluid power technicians deal with equipment that uses the pressure of a liquid or gas in a closed container to transmit, multiply, or control power. Working under the supervision of an engineer or engineering staff, they assemble, install, maintain, and test fluid power equipment, which is found in almost every facet of American daily life.

History

Machinery that operates on fluid power has been used for thousands

of years. In Roman times, water flowing past a rotating paddle wheel was used to produce power for milling. Early leather bellows, hand-operated by blacksmiths, were the first known devices to use compressed air. In Italy, in the 16th century, a more sophisticated bellows was invented that used falling water to compress air. Shortly thereafter, Denis Papin, a French physicist, used power from a waterwheel to compress air in a similar manner.

The 19th century brought the first practical application of an air-driven, piston-operated hammer, invented in Great Britain by George Law. In the mid-1800s, water-cooled reciprocating compressors were introduced in the United States and resulted in the development of large compressed-air units that factory workers used to operate industrial tools. In 1875, American engineer and industrialist George Westinghouse created and utilized a continuous automatic compressed-air brake system for trains.

In the latter part of the 19th century and the early part of the 20th, experiments in fluid dynamics by Osborne Reynolds and Ludwig Prandtl led to a new understanding of the way fluid behaves in certain circumstances. These findings laid the groundwork for modern fluid power mechanics. The 20th and 21st centuries have witnessed a significant increase in the use of fluid power for many different purposes.

Fluid power workers are now employed in any number of industries, from aerospace to materials handling. Fluid power is also routinely used and depended upon in almost everyone's daily life. Anyone who has ever ridden in a car, for example, has relied upon fluid power to operate the car's hydraulic braking system. With fluid power so widely used, literally thousands of businesses throughout the United States employ men and women who are trained in its various aspects. Fluid power technicians, with their specialized skills and knowledge, have become a mainstay of industrial support groups that work with this type of machinery.

The Job

Many different machines use some kind of fluid power system, including equipment used in industries such as agriculture, manufacturing, defense, and mining. We come across fluid power systems every day when we use automatic door closers, bicycle pumps, and spray guns. Even automobile transmissions incorporate fluid power.

There are two types of fluid power machines. The first kind—hydraulic machines—use water, oil, or another liquid in a closed system to transmit the energy needed to do work. For example, a hydraulic jack, which can be used to lift heavy loads, is a cylinder with a piston fitted inside it. When a liquid is pumped into the bottom of the cylinder, the piston is forced upward, lifting the weight on the jack. To lower the weight, the liquid is released through a valve, returning the pressure in the system to normal.

Pneumatic machines, the other type of fluid power systems, are activated by the pressure of air or another gas in a closed system. Pavement-breaking jackhammers and compressed-air paint sprayers are common examples of pneumatic machines.

Fluid power systems are a part of most machines used in industry, so fluid power technicians work in many different settings. Most often, however, they work in factories where fluid power systems are used in manufacturing. In such a factory, for example, they might maintain and service pneumatic machines that bolt together products on an automated assembly line.

In their work, fluid power technicians analyze blueprints, drawings, and specifications; set up various milling, shaping, grinding, and drilling machines; make precision parts; use sensitive measuring instruments to make sure the parts are exactly the required size; and use hand and power tools to put together components of the fluid power system they are assembling or repairing.

Technicians may also be responsible for testing fluid power systems. To determine whether a piece of equipment is working properly, they connect the unit to test equipment that measures such factors as fluid pressure, flow rates, and power loss from friction or wear. Based on their analysis of the test results, they may advise changes in the equipment setup or instrumentation.

Some technicians work for companies that are researching better ways to develop and use fluid power systems. They may work in laboratories as part of research and development teams who set up fluid power equipment and test it under operating conditions. Other technicians work as sales and service representatives for companies that make and sell fluid power equipment to industrial plants. These technicians travel from one plant to another, providing customers with specialized information and assistance with their equipment. Some technicians repair and maintain fluid power components of heavy equipment used in construction, on farms, or in mining. Because fluid power technology is important in the flight controls, landing gear, and brakes of airplanes, many technicians are also employed in the aircraft industry.

Requirements

HIGH SCHOOL

If you are considering a career in fluid power, you should take as many courses as possible in computer science and mathematics. Physics, shop, drafting, and English will also provide a solid background for this type of work.

POSTSECONDARY TRAINING

In the past, you could become a fluid power technician with only a high school diploma and, perhaps, some related technical experience.

Technicians were trained in fluid power technology by their employers or by taking short courses or workshops. Today, however, most employers prefer to hire fluid power technicians who have at least two years of post-high school training, such as that offered by community and technical colleges.

There are relatively few technical training programs that focus primarily on fluid power technology—fewer than 30 in the entire United States. A student enrolled in one of these programs might expect to take classes on very specialized topics, such as fluid power math, process and fabrication fundamentals, hydraulic components and accessories, pneumatic components and circuits, and advanced systems calculations. If it is not possible to attend one of the schools that offers programs in fluid power, training in a related field, such as mechanical or electrical technology, can provide adequate preparation for employment.

CERTIFICATION OR LICENSING
Certification for fluid power technicians is voluntary. Offered through the Fluid Power Certification Board, the certification process is administered by the Fluid Power Society. Applicants must attend two or more days of classes and pass a three-hour written examination before receiving technician certification. This certification may be beneficial to technicians in finding jobs, obtaining more advanced positions, or receiving higher pay.

OTHER REQUIREMENTS
Technicians must be able to understand and analyze mechanical systems. In order to do this well, they should have both mechanical aptitude and an analytical mindset. Because they often work on teams, an ability to work well and communicate easily with others is important. Finally, a successful technician should enjoy challenges and the troubleshooting of problems.

Exploring

Your school or public library should have books that explain the field of fluid power. If you happen to live near one of the schools that offers a degree in fluid power technology, it may be possible to arrange a meeting with instructors or students in the program. Talking with someone who is already employed as a fluid power technician can be an excellent way of learning about the job firsthand. Finally, taking certain classes, such as machine shop, physics, or electronics, might help you gauge your enjoyment and ability level for this work.

Employers

The largest consumers of fluid power products are the aerospace, construction equipment, agricultural equipment, machine tool, and material handling industries, according to the National Fluid Power Association, an industry trade organization. Fluid power also provides power for auxiliary systems on planes, ships, trains, and trucks.

Starting Out

Most fluid power technicians obtain their jobs through their community and technical college placement offices. In addition, organizations such as the Fluid Power Society and the Fluid Power Educational Foundation have lists of their corporate members that can be used to start a job search. Some openings might be listed in the employment sections of newspapers.

Advancement

Some technicians advance simply by becoming more knowledgeable and skilled in their work and eventually receive more responsibility. Another route for technicians is to become a *fluid power specialist* by taking additional training and upgrading their certification. A specialist designs and applies systems and can instruct newer employees on the basics of fluid power systems.

Some technicians go into sales and marketing, using their experience and knowledge to provide customers with technical assistance. Another option is to become a *fluid power consultant*, who works with different companies to analyze, design, or improve fluid power systems.

Earnings

Salaries for fluid power technicians vary according to geographic location and industry. A Fluid Power Educational Foundation survey reports that college graduates (of both two- and four-year programs) earned starting salaries that ranged from $35,000 to $39,000 in 1999. An estimated national average wage for technicians might be in the low to mid-$40,000s. Those who move into consulting or other advanced positions can earn even more. Most workers in this field receive a full benefits package, often including vacation days, sick leave, medical and life insurance, and a retirement plan.

Work Environment

Because fluid power technicians work in any number of different industries, their work environments vary. Many work in industrial settings and must spend much of their time on the manufacturing floor. In this case, they may have to become accustomed to noise and heat generated by the machinery, although the industry is addressing the noise level issue. Others work in laboratories or testing facilities. Those involved in sales and marketing or in installing and repairing equipment may travel to different customer locations.

The work is frequently dirty, as technicians often have to handle machinery that has been used and may be leaking fluid. Also, working on large machinery and components requires physical strength and may require being in areas where safety regulations must be followed.

Many workers in this field find their jobs enjoyable and satisfying. Because they deal with different problems and solutions all the time, the work is challenging, interesting, and not repetitious. It can also be gratifying to figure out how to make a machine run properly or improve upon its performance through testing and experimenting.

Outlook

Because fluid power is used in so many different industries, the need for technicians is growing rapidly. Currently, in fact, the demand for these trained workers exceeds the supply. In the 1990s, electrohydraulic and electropneumatic technologies opened up new markets, such as active suspensions on automobiles, and reestablished older markets, such as robotics. Therefore, the fluid power industry is expected to continue growing, and the outlook for technicians should remain strong through the next decade.

For More Information

For a list of schools offering courses in fluid power technology and information about available scholarships, contact:
FLUID POWER EDUCATIONAL FOUNDATION
3333 North Mayfair Road, Suite 101
Milwaukee, WI 53222
Tel: 414-778-3364
Web: http://www.fpef.org

For information on certification, contact:
FLUID POWER SOCIETY
3245 Freemansburg Avenue
Palmer, PA 18045-7118
Tel: 800-303-8520
Email: info@ifps.org
Web: http://www.ifps.org

For career information and job listings, contact:
NATIONAL FLUID POWER ASSOCIATION
3333 North Mayfair Road
Milwaukee, WI 53222-3219
Tel: 414-778-3344
Email: nfpa@nfpa.com
Web: http://www.nfpa.com

General Maintenance Mechanics

Quick Facts

School Subjects
Mathematics
Technical/shop

Personal Skills
Mechanical/manipulative
Technical/scientific

Work Environment
Indoors and outdoors
Primarily one location

Minimum Education Level
High school diploma

Salary Range
$16,307 to $27,851 to $44,574

Certification or Licensing
Voluntary

Outlook
Little change or more slowly than
the average

Overview

General maintenance mechanics, sometimes called *maintenance technicians,* repair and maintain machines, mechanical equipment, and buildings and work on plumbing, electrical, and controls. They also do minor construction or carpentry work and routine preventive maintenance to keep the physical structures of businesses, schools, factories, and apartment buildings in good condition. They also maintain and repair specialized equipment and machinery found in cafeterias, laundries, hospitals, offices, and factories.

History

Before machines came to dominate the manufacturing of goods, crafts workers had to learn many different kinds of skills. Blacksmiths, for example, had to know about forging techniques, horseshoeing, making decorative metalwork, and many other aspects of their trade. Carriage makers had to be familiar with carpentry, metalworking, wheel-making, upholstering, and design.

The Industrial Revolution set in motion many new trends, however, including a shift toward factory-type settings with workers who specialized in specific functions. This shift occurred partly because new machine production methods required a high degree of discipline and organization. Another reason for the change was because the new technology was so complex no one person could be expected to master a whole field and keep up with changes that developed in it.

In a way, today's general maintenance mechanics recall crafts workers of the era before specialization. They are jacks-of-all-trades. Typically they have a reasonable amount of skill in a variety of fields, including construction, electrical work, carpentry, plumbing, machining, and direct digital controls, as well as other trades. They are responsible for keeping buildings and machines in good working order. In order to do this, they must have a broad understanding of mechanical tools and processes as well as the ability to apply their knowledge to solving problems. Today there are over 1.6 million general maintenance mechanics employed in the United States, working in almost every industry.

The Job

General maintenance mechanics perform almost any task that may be required to maintain a building or the equipment in it. They may be called on to replace faulty electrical outlets, fix air-conditioning motors, install water lines, build partitions, patch plaster or drywall, open clogged drains, dismantle, clean, and oil machinery, paint windows, doors, and woodwork, repair institutional-size dishwashers or laundry machines, and see to many other problems. Because of the diverse nature of the responsibilities of maintenance mechanics, they have to know how to use a variety of materials and be skilled in the use of most hand tools and ordinary power tools. They also must be able to recognize when they cannot handle a problem and must recommend that a specialized technician be called.

General maintenance mechanics work in many kinds of settings. Mechanics who work primarily on keeping industrial machines in good condition may be called *factory maintenance workers* or *mill maintenance workers*, while those mechanics who concentrate on the maintenance of a building's physical structure may be called *building maintenance workers and technicians*.

Once a problem or defect has been identified and diagnosed, maintenance mechanics must plan the repairs. They may consult blueprints, repair manuals, and parts catalogs to determine what to do. They obtain supplies and new parts from a storeroom or order them from a distributor. They install new parts in place of worn or broken ones, using hand tools, power tools, and sometimes electronic test devices and other specialized equipment. In some situations, maintenance mechanics may fix an old part or even fabricate a new part. To do this, they may need to set up and operate machine tools, such as lathes or milling machines, and operate gas- or arc-welding equipment to join metal parts together.

One of the most important kinds of duties general maintenance mechanics perform is routine preventive maintenance to correct defects before machinery breaks down or a building begins to deteriorate. This type of maintenance keeps small problems from turning into large, expensive ones. Mechanics often inspect machinery on a regular schedule, perhaps following a checklist that includes such items as inspecting belts, checking fluid levels, replacing filters, oiling moving parts, and so forth. They keep records of the repair work done and the inspection dates. Repair and inspection records can be important evidence of compliance with insurance requirements and government safety regulations.

New buildings often have computer-controlled systems, so mechanics who work in them must have basic computer skills. For example, newer buildings might have light sensors that are electronically controlled and automatically turn lights on and off. The maintenance mechanic has to understand how to make adjustments and repairs.

In small establishments, one mechanic may be the only person working in maintenance, and thus he or she may be responsible for almost any kind of repair. In large establishments, however, tasks may be divided among several mechanics. For example, one mechanic may be assigned to install and set up new equipment, while another may handle preventive maintenance.

Requirements

HIGH SCHOOL
Many employers prefer to hire helpers or mechanics who are high school graduates, but a diploma is not always required. High school courses that provide good preparation for this occupation include mechanical drawing, metal shop, electrical shop, woodworking, blueprint reading, general science, and applied mathematics.

POSTSECONDARY TRAINING

Some mechanics learn their skills by working as helpers to people employed in building trades, such as electricians or carpenters. Other mechanics attend trade or vocational schools that teach many of the necessary skills. Becoming fully qualified for a mechanic's job usually requires one to four years of on-the-job training or classroom instruction, or some combination of both.

CERTIFICATION OR LICENSING

There are some certification and training programs open to maintenance mechanics. The BOMI Institute, for example, offers the designation of Systems Maintenance Technician (SMT) to applicants who have completed courses in boilers, heating systems, and applied mathematics; refrigeration systems and accessories; air handling, water treatment, and plumbing systems; electrical and illumination systems; and building control systems. Technicians who have achieved SMT status can go on and become certified as Systems Maintenance Administrators by taking further classes in building design and maintenance, energy management, and supervision. While not necessarily required for employment, employees with certification may become more valuable assets to their employers and may have better chances at advancement.

OTHER REQUIREMENTS

General maintenance mechanics need to have good manual dexterity and mechanical aptitude. People who enjoy taking things apart and putting them back together are good candidates for this position. Since some of the work, such as reaching, squatting, and lifting, requires physical strength and stamina, reasonably good health is necessary. Mechanics also need the ability to analyze and solve problems and to work effectively on their own without constant supervision.

Exploring

Shop classes can give you a good indication of your mechanical aptitude and of whether or not you would enjoy maintenance work. The best way to experience the work these mechanics do, however, is to get a summer or part-time job as a maintenance helper in a factory, apartment complex, or similar setting. If such a job is not available, you might try talking with a maintenance mechanic to get a fuller, more complete picture of his or her responsibilities.

Employers

General maintenance mechanics are employed in factories, hospitals, schools, colleges, hotels, offices, stores, malls, gas and electric companies, government agencies, and apartment buildings throughout the United States. Statistics from the U.S. Bureau of Labor Statistics indicate that there are over 1.6 million people in the field. Approximately one-third are employed in manufacturing industries. Others are employed in service industries, such as elementary and secondary schools, colleges and universities, hospitals and nursing homes, hotels, office and apartment buildings, government agencies, and utility companies.

Starting Out

General maintenance mechanics usually start as helpers to experienced mechanics and learn their skills on the job. Beginning helpers are given the simplest jobs, such as changing light bulbs or making minor drywall repairs. As general maintenance mechanics acquire skills, they are assigned more complicated work, such as troubleshooting malfunctioning machinery.

Job seekers in this field usually apply directly to potential employers. Information on job openings for mechanic's helpers can often be found through newspaper classified ads, school placement offices, and the local offices of the state employment service. Graduates of trade or vocational schools may be able to get referrals and information from their school's placement office. Union offices may also be a good place to learn about job opportunities.

Advancement

Some general maintenance mechanics who are employed in large organizations may advance to supervisory positions. Another possibility is to move into one of the traditional building trades and become a crafts worker, such as a plumber or electrician. In smaller organizations, promotion opportunities are limited, although increases in pay may result from an employee's good performance and increased value to the employer.

Earnings

Earnings for general maintenance mechanics vary widely depending on skill, geographic location, and industry. The *Occupational Outlook Handbook* reports that general maintenance mechanics and repairers earned a median hourly wage of $13.39 in 2000. Earnings ranged from $7.84 to $21.43 an hour.

Almost all maintenance mechanics receive a benefits package that includes health insurance, paid vacation, sick leave, and a retirement plan. Mechanics earn overtime pay for work in excess of 40 hours per week.

Work Environment

General maintenance mechanics work in almost every industry and in a wide variety of facilities. In most cases, they work a 40-hour week. Some work evening or night shifts or on weekends; they may also be on call for emergency repairs. In the course of a single day, mechanics may do a variety of tasks in different parts of a building or in several buildings, and they may encounter different conditions in each spot. Sometimes they have to work in hot or cold conditions, on ladders, in awkward or cramped positions, among noisy machines, or in other uncomfortable places. Sometimes they must lift heavy weights. On the job, they must stay aware of potential hazards such as electrical shocks, burns, falls, and cuts and bruises. By following safety regulations and using tools properly, they can keep such risks to a minimum.

The mechanic who works in a small establishment may be the only maintenance worker and is often responsible for doing his or her job with little direct supervision. Those who work in larger establishments usually report to a maintenance supervisor who assigns tasks and directs their activities.

Outlook

Employment of general maintenance mechanics is expected to grow more slowly than the average through 2010. Although the rate of construction of new apartment and office buildings, factories, hotels, schools, and stores is expected to be slower than in the past, most of these facilities still require the services of maintenance mechanics. This is a large occupation with a high turnover rate. In addition to newly created jobs, many openings will arise as experienced mechanics transfer to other occupations or leave the labor force.

General maintenance mechanics who work for manufacturing companies may be subject to layoffs during bad economic times, when their employers are under pressure to cut costs. Most mechanics, however, are not usually as vulnerable to layoffs related to economic conditions.

For More Information

This nonprofit organization provides education programs for commercial property professionals, including building engineers and technicians.
BUILDING OWNERS AND MANAGERS ASSOCIATION
1201 New York Avenue, NW, Suite 300
Washington, DC 20005
Tel: 202-408-2662
Web: http://www.boma.org

BOMI INSTITUTE
1521 Ritchie Highway
Arnold, MD 21012
Tel: 800-235-2664
Email: careers@bomi-edu.org
Web: http://www.bomi-edu.org

For information on general maintenance careers in building maintenance and construction, contact:
MECHANICAL CONTRACTORS ASSOCIATION OF AMERICA
1385 Piccard Drive
Rockville, MD 20850
Tel: 301-869-5800
Web: http://www.mcaa.org/careers

Industrial Machinery Mechanics

Overview

Industrial machinery mechanics, often called *machinery maintenance mechanics* or *industrial machinery repairers,* inspect, maintain, repair, and adjust industrial production and processing machinery and equipment to ensure its proper operation in various industries.

History

Before 1750 and the beginning of the Industrial Revolution in Europe, almost all work was done by hand. Families grew their own food, wove their own cloth, and bought or traded very little.

Quick Facts

School Subjects
  Mathematics
  Technical/shop
Personal Skills
  Mechanical/manipulative
  Technical/scientific
Work Environment
  Primarily indoors
  Primarily one location
Minimum Education Level
  Apprenticeship
Salary Range
  $23,525 to $35,984 to $54,621+
Certification or Licensing
  None available
Outlook
  Little change or more slowly than
  the average

Gradually the economic landscape changed. Factories mass-produced products that had once been created by hand. The spinning jenny, a multiple-spindle machine for spinning wool or cotton, was one of the first machines of the Industrial Revolution. After it came a long procession of inventions and developments, including the steam engine, power loom, cotton gin, steamboat, locomotive, telegraph, and Bessemer converter. With these machines came the need for people who could maintain and repair them.

Mechanics learned that all machines are based on six configurations: the lever, the wheel and axle, the pulley, the inclined plane, the wedge, and the screw. By combining these elements in more complex ways, the machines could do more work in less time than people or animals could do. Thus, the role of machinery mechanics became vital in keeping production lines running and businesses profitable.

The Industrial Revolution continues even today, although now it is known as the Age of Automation. As machines become more numerous and more complex, the work of the industrial machinery mechanic becomes even more necessary.

The Job

The types of machinery on which industrial machinery mechanics work are as varied as the types of industries operating in the United States today. Mechanics are employed in metal stamping plants, printing plants, chemical and plastics plants, and almost any type of large-scale industrial operation that can be imagined. The machinery in these plants must be maintained regularly. Breakdowns and delays with one machine can hinder a plant's entire operation, which is costly for the company.

Preventive maintenance is a major part of mechanics' jobs. They inspect the equipment, oil and grease moving components, and clean and repair parts. They also keep detailed maintenance records on the equipment they service. They often follow blueprints and engineering specifications to maintain and fix equipment.

When breakdowns occur, mechanics may partially or completely disassemble a machine to make the necessary repairs. They replace worn bearings, adjust clutches, and replace and repair defective parts. They may have to order replacement parts from the machinery's manufacturer. If no parts are available, they may have to make the necessary replacements, using milling machines, lathes, or other tooling equipment. After the machine is reassembled, they may have to make adjustments to its operational settings. They often work with the machine's regular operator to test it. When repairing electronically controlled machinery, mechanics may work closely with electronic repairers or electricians who maintain the machine's electronic parts.

Often these mechanics can identify potential breakdowns and fix problems before any real damage or delays occur. They may notice that a machine is vibrating, rattling, or squeaking, or they may see that the items produced by the machine are flawed. Many types of new machinery are built with programmed internal evaluation systems that check the accuracy and condition of equipment. This assists mechanics in their jobs, but it also makes them responsible for maintaining the checkup systems.

Machinery installations are becoming another facet of a mechanic's job. As plants retool and invest in new equipment, they rely on mechanics to properly situate and install the machinery. In many plants, millwrights traditionally did this job, but as employers increasingly seek workers with multiple skills, industrial machinery mechanics are taking on new responsibilities.

Industrial machinery mechanics use a wide range of tools when doing preventive maintenance or making repairs. For example, they may use simple tools such as a screwdriver and wrench to repair an engine or a hoist to lift a printing press off the ground. Sometimes they solder or weld equipment. They use power and hand tools and precision measuring instruments. In some shops, mechanics troubleshoot for the entire plant's operations. Others may become experts in electronics, hydraulics, pneumatics, or other specialties.

Requirements

HIGH SCHOOL
While most employers prefer to hire those who have completed high school, opportunities do exist for those without a diploma as long as they have had some kind of related training. While you are in high school, take courses in mechanical drawing, general mathematics, algebra, and geometry. Other classes that will help prepare you for this career are physics, computers, and electronics. Any class that gives you experience in blueprint reading adds to your qualifications.

POSTSECONDARY TRAINING
In the past, most industrial machinery mechanics learned the skills of the trade informally by spending several years as helpers in a particular factory. Currently, as machinery has become more complex, more formal training is necessary. Today many mechanics learn the trade through apprenticeship programs sponsored by a local trade union. Apprenticeship programs usually last four years and include both on-the-job and related classroom training. In addition to the use and care of machine and hand tools, apprentices learn the operation, lubrication, and adjustment of the machinery and equipment they will maintain. In class they learn shop mathematics, blueprint reading, safety, hydraulics, welding, and other subjects related to the trade.

Students may also obtain training through vocational or technical schools. Useful programs are those that offer machine shop courses and provide training in electronics and numerical control machine tools.

OTHER REQUIREMENTS
Students interested in this field should possess mechanical aptitude and manual dexterity. Good physical condition and agility are necessary because as a mechanic you will sometimes have to lift heavy objects, crawl under large machines, or climb to reach equipment located high above the factory floor.

Mechanics are responsible for valuable equipment and are often called upon to exercise considerable independent judgment. Because of technological advances, you should be willing to learn the requirements of new machines and production techniques. When a plant purchases new equipment, the equipment's manufacturer often trains plant employees in proper operation and maintenance. Technological change requires mechanics to have adaptability and inquiring minds.

Exploring

If you are interested in this field, you should take as many shop courses as you can. Exploring and repairing machinery, such as automobiles and home appliances, will also sharpen your skills. In addition, try landing part-time work or a summer job in an industrial plant that gives you the opportunity to observe industrial repair work being done.

Employers

Industrial machinery mechanics work in a wide variety of plants and are employed in every part of the country, although employment is concentrated in industrialized areas. According to the U.S. Department of Labor, one-third of industrial machinery mechanics work in industries such as chemicals, food processing, textile mill products, primary metals, and fabricated metal products. Others work for public utilities, government agencies, and mining companies.

Starting Out

Jobs can be obtained by applying directly to companies that use industrial equipment or machinery. The majority of mechanics work for manufacturing plants. These plants are found in a wide variety of industries, including the automotive, plastics, textile, electronics, packaging, food, beverage, and aerospace industries. Chances for job openings may be better at a large plant. New workers are generally assigned to work as helpers or trainees.

Prospective mechanics also may learn of job openings or apprenticeship programs through local unions. Industrial mechanics may be represented by one of several unions, depending on their industry and place of employment. These unions include the International Union, United Automobile, Aerospace, and Agricultural Implement Workers of America; the United Steelworkers of America; the International Union of Electronic, Electrical, Salaried, Machine, and Furniture Workers; and the International Association of Machinists and Aerospace Workers. Private and state employment offices are other good sources of job openings.

Advancement

Those who begin as helpers or trainees usually become journeymen in four years. Although opportunities for advancement beyond this rank are somewhat limited, industrial machinery mechanics who learn more complicated machinery and equipment can advance into higher-paying positions. The most highly skilled mechanics may be promoted to master mechanics. Those who demonstrate good leadership and interpersonal skills can become supervisors. Skilled mechanics also have the option of becoming machinists, numerical control tool programmers, precision metalworkers, packaging machinery technicians, or robotics technicians. Some of these positions do require additional training, but the skills of a mechanic transfer readily to these areas.

Earnings

In 2000, median hourly earnings for industrial machinery mechanics were $17.30, according to the U.S. Department of Labor. The lowest-paid 10 percent earned less than $11.31 an hour. The highest-paid 10 percent earned $26.26 or more per hour. Apprentices generally earn lower wages and earn incremental raises as they advance in their training. Earnings vary based on experience, skills, type of industry, and geographic location. For example, mechanics employed in the textile industry generally earn wages at the low end of the scale, with workers in the automotive, metalworking, and aircraft industries earning wages at the high end. Mechanics in the Midwest typically earn higher salaries than those in the South. Those working in union plants generally earn more than those in nonunion plants. Most industrial machinery mechanics are provided with benefit packages, which can include paid holidays and vacations; medical, dental, and life insurance; and retirement plans.

Work Environment

Industrial machinery mechanics work in all types of manufacturing plants, which may be hot, noisy, and dirty or relatively quiet and clean. Mechanics frequently work with greasy, dirty equipment and need to be able to adapt to a variety of physical conditions. Because machinery is not always accessible, mechanics may have to work in stooped or cramped positions or on high ladders.

Although working around machinery poses some danger, this risk is minimized with proper safety precautions. Modern machinery includes many safety features and devices, and most plants follow good safety practices. Mechanics often wear protective clothing and equipment, such as hard hats and safety belts, glasses, and shoes.

Mechanics work with little supervision and need to be able to work well with others. They need to be flexible and respond to changing priorities, which can result in interruptions that pull a mechanic off one job to repair a more urgent problem. Although the standard workweek is 40 hours, overtime is common. Because factories and other sites cannot afford breakdowns, industrial machinery mechanics may be called to the plant at night or on weekends for emergency repairs.

Outlook

The U.S. Department of Labor predicts that employment will grow more slowly than the average through 2010 for industrial machinery mechanics. Some industries will have a greater need for mechanics than others. Much of the new automated production equipment that companies are purchasing has its own self-diagnostic capabilities and is more reliable than older equipment. Although this machinery still needs to be maintained, most job openings will stem from the replacement of transferring or retiring workers.

Certain industries are extremely susceptible to changing economic factors and reduce production activities in slow periods. During these periods, companies may lay off workers or reduce hours. Mechanics are less likely to be laid off than other workers, as machines need to be maintained regardless of production levels. Slower production periods and temporary shutdowns are often used to overhaul equipment. Nonetheless, employment opportunities are generally better at companies experiencing growth or stable levels of production.

Because machinery is becoming more complex and automated, mechanics need to be more highly skilled than in the past. Mechanics who stay up to date with new technologies, particularly those related to electronics and computers, should find favorable employment opportunities over the next decade.

For More Information

For information about apprentice programs, contact the UAW.
INTERNATIONAL UNION, UNITED AUTOMOBILE, AEROSPACE, AND AGRICULTURAL IMPLEMENT WORKERS OF AMERICA (UAW)
8000 East Jefferson Avenue
Detroit, MI 48214
Tel: 313-926-5000
Web: http://www.uaw.org

For information about the machining industry and career opportunities, contact:
NATIONAL TOOLING AND MACHINING ASSOCIATION
9300 Livingston Road
Fort Washington, MD 20744
Tel: 301-248-6200
Web: http://www.ntma.org

For career information, contact:
PRECISION MACHINED PRODUCTS ASSOCIATION
6700 West Snowville Road
Brecksville, OH 44141
Web: http://www.pmpa.org

Instrumentation Technicians

Quick Facts

School Subjects
  Mathematics
  Physics
  Technical/shop
Personal Skills
  Mechanical/manipulative
  Technical/scientific
Work Environment
  Primarily indoors
  Primarily one location
Minimum Education Level
  Associate's degree
Salary Range
  $16,500 to $48,600 to $69,700
Certification or Licensing
  Voluntary
Outlook
  About as fast as the average

Overview

Instrumentation technicians are skilled craft workers who do precision work and are involved in the field of measurement and control. Technicians inspect, test, repair, and adjust instruments that detect, measure, and record changes in industrial environments. They work with theoretical or analytical problems, helping engineers improve instrument and system performance.

History

The use of instruments as a means for people to monitor and control their environment and to guide their activities is as old as the sundial. As modern technology progresses, we still find ourselves in need of precise information that is sometimes difficult for a person to physically obtain.

For instance, with the advent of the steam engine in the 19th century, a train operator had to know how much pressure was inside a boiler. A gauge was designed to measure this safely. The early 20th century saw the development of the internal combustion engine and powered flight. With these developments, engineers and technicians designed and made instruments such as speedometers, altimeters, and tachometers to provide vital data for the safe operation of these engines and auxiliary equipment.

Since World War II, instrumentation technology has become a fast-growing field, responding to challenging needs as people explore space, research our oceans, perform biomedical studies, and advance nuclear technology. Today, instrumentation technology involves both measurement and control, and technicians are critical to their accurate operation. For instance, technicians at nuclear reactors assure that the devices inside accurately measure heat, pressure, and radiation and their rates of change. If any of these factors is not at its specific level, then other instruments make the necessary adjustments. The plant operates safely and efficiently.

The Job

Instrumentation technicians work with complex instruments that detect, measure, and record changes in industrial environments. As part of their duties, these technicians perform tests, develop new instruments, and install, repair, inspect, and maintain the instruments. Examples of such instruments include altimeters, pressure gauges, speedometers, and radiation detection devices.

Some instrumentation technicians operate the laboratory equipment that produces or records the effects of certain conditions on the test instruments, such as vibration, stress, temperature, humidity, pressure, altitude, and acceleration. Other technicians sketch, build, and modify electronic and mechanical fixtures, instruments, and related apparatus.

As part of their duties, technicians might verify the dimensions and functions of devices assembled by other technicians and craft workers, plan test programs, and direct technical personnel in carrying out these tests. Instrumentation technicians also often perform mathematical calculations on instrument readings and test results so they can be used in graphs and written reports.

Instrumentation technicians work with three major categories of instruments: *pneumatic and electropneumatic equipment,* which includes temperature and flow transmitters and receivers and devices that start or are started by such things as pressure springs, diaphragms, and bellows; *hydraulic instrumentation,* which includes hydraulic valves, hydraulic valve operators, and electrohydraulic equipment; and *electrical and electronic equipment,* which includes electrical sensing elements and transducers, electronic recorders, electronic telemetering systems, and electronic computers.

In some industries, a technician might work on equipment from each category, while in other industries, a technician might be responsible for only one specific type of task. The different levels of responsibility depend also on the instrumentation technician's level of training and experience.

Instrumentation technicians may hold a variety of different positions. *Mechanical instrumentation technicians,* for example, handle routine mechanical functions. They check out equipment before operation, calibrate it during operation, rebuild it using standard replacement parts, mount interconnecting equipment from blueprints, and perform routine repairs using common hand tools. They must be able to read both instrumentation and electronic schematic diagrams. *Instrumentation repair technicians* determine the causes of malfunctions and make repairs. Such repairs usually involve individual pieces of equipment, as distinguished from entire systems. This job requires experience, primarily laboratory-oriented, beyond that of mechanical instrumentation technicians.

Troubleshooting instrumentation technicians make adjustments to instruments and control systems, calibrate equipment, set up tests, diagnose malfunctions, and revise existing systems. Their work is performed either on-site or at a workbench. Advanced training in mathematics, physics, and graphics is required for this level of work. Technicians who are involved in the design of instruments are *instrumentation design technicians.* They work under the supervision of a design engineer. Using information prepared by engineers, they build models and prototypes and prepare sketches, working drawings, and diagrams. These technicians also test out new system designs, order parts, and make mock-ups of new systems.

Technicians in certain industries have more specialized duties and responsibilities. *Biomedical equipment technicians* work with instruments used during medical procedures. They receive special training in the biomedical area in which their instruments are used. (See the article Biomedical Equipment Technicians.) *Calibration technicians,* also known as *standards laboratory technicians,* work in the electronics industry and in aerospace and aircraft manufacturing. As part of their inspection of systems and instruments, they measure parts for conformity to specifications, and they help develop calibration standards, devise formulas to solve problems in measurement and calibration, and write procedures and practical guides for other calibration technicians.

Electromechanical technicians work with automated mechanical equipment controlled by electronic sensing devices. They assist mechanical engineers in the design and development of such equipment, analyze test results, and write reports. The technician follows blueprints, operates metalworking machines, builds instrument housings, installs electrical equipment, and calibrates instruments and machinery. Technicians who specialize in the assembly of prototype instruments are known as *development technicians. Fabrication technicians* specialize in the assembly of production instruments.

Nuclear instrumentation technicians work with instruments at a nuclear power plant. These instruments control the various systems within the nuclear reactor, detect radiation, and sound alarms in case of equipment failure. *Instrument sales technicians* work for equipment manufacturing companies. They analyze customer needs, outline specifications for equipment cost and function, and sometimes do emergency troubleshooting.

Requirements

HIGH SCHOOL
Math and science courses, such as algebra, geometry, physics, and chemistry, are essential prerequisites to becoming an instrument technician. In addition, machine and electrical shop courses will help you become familiar with electrical, mechanical, and electronic technology. Classes in mechanical drawing and computer-aided drafting are also beneficial. Instrumentation technicians also need good writing and communication skills and should take English, composition, and speech classes.

POSTSECONDARY TRAINING
The basic requirement for an entry-level job is completion of a two-year technical program or equivalent experience in a related field. Such equivalent experience may come from work in an electronics or manufacturing firm or any job that provides experience working with mechanical or electrical equipment.

Technical programs beyond high school can be found in community colleges as well as technical schools. Programs are offered in many different disciplines in addition to instrumentation technology. Programs may be in electronics or in electrical, mechanical, biomedical, or nuclear technology.

Most programs allow technicians to develop hands-on and laboratory skills as well as learn theory. Classes are likely to include instruction on electronic circuitry, computer science, mathematics, and physics. Courses in basic electronics, electrical theory, and graphics are also important. Technical writing is helpful, as most technicians will prepare technical reports. Industrial economics, applied psychology, and plant management courses are helpful to those who plan to move into customer service or design.

CERTIFICATION OR LICENSING
Instrumentation technicians who graduate from a recognized technical program may become certified by the National Institute for Certification in Engineering Technologies, although this is usually not a required part of a job. Certification is available at various levels, each combining a written exam in one of over 30 specialty fields with a specified amount of job-related experience. Technicians are also eligible to become members of the International Society for Measurement and Control, which offers an accreditation. Membership in professional organizations is optional but is encouraged as a means of keeping abreast of advancing technology.

OTHER REQUIREMENTS
Successful instrumentation technicians need mathematical and scientific aptitudes and the patience to methodically pursue complex questions. A tolerance for following prescribed procedures is essential, especially when undertaking assignments requiring a very precise, unchanging system of problem solving. Successful instrumentation technicians are able to provide solutions quickly and accurately even in stressful situations.

Exploring

As a way to test your abilities and learn more about calibration work, you could build small electronic equipment. Kits for building radios and other small appliances are available in some electronics shops. This gives some basic understanding of electronic components and applications.

Some communities and schools also have clubs for people interested in electronics. They may offer classes that would teach you basic skills in construction, repair, and adjustment of electrical and electronic products. Model building, particularly in hard plastic and steel, will give you a good understanding of how to adapt and fit parts together. It may also help develop hand skills if you want to work with precision instruments.

Visits to industrial laboratories, instrument shops, research laboratories, power installations, and manufacturing companies that rely on automated processes can give you a glimpse of the activities of instrumentation technicians. During such visits, you might be able to speak with technicians about their work or with employers about possible openings in their company. Also, you might look into getting a summer or part-time job as a helper on an industrial maintenance crew.

Employers

Employers of instrumentation technicians include oil refineries, chemical and industrial laboratories, electronics firms, aircraft and aeronautical manufacturers, and biomedical firms. Companies involved in space exploration, oceanographic research, and national defense systems also use technicians. In addition, they work in various capacities in such industries as automotives, food, metals, ceramics, pulp and paper, power, textiles, pharmaceuticals, mining, metals, and pollution control.

Starting Out

Many companies recruit students prior to their graduation. Chemical and medical research companies especially need maintenance and operations technicians and usually recruit at schools where training in these areas is strong. Similarly, many industries in search of design technicians recruit at technical institutes and community colleges, where the program is likely to meet their needs.

Students may also get assistance in their job searches through their schools' job placement services, or they may learn about openings through ads in the newspapers. Prospective employees can also apply directly to a company in which they are interested.

Advancement

Entry-level technicians develop their skills by learning tasks on their employers' equipment. Those with good academic records may, upon completion of an employer's basic program, move to an advanced level in sales or another area where a general understanding of the field is more important than specific laboratory skills. Technicians who have developed proficiency in instrumentation may choose to move to a supervisory or specialized position that requires knowledge of a particular aspect of instrumentation.

Earnings

Earnings for instrumentation technicians vary by industry, geographic region, educational background, experience, and level of responsibility. According to the U.S. Bureau of Labor Statistics, median annual earnings of instrumentation technicians in the aerospace industry were $48,600 in 2000. Electrical and electronic engineering technicians had median annual earnings of $40,020. Electromechanical technicians earned a median of $36,150, and mechanical engineering technicians earned $39,570. Repairers of electrical and electronics instruments for commercial and industrial equipment earned about $36,910. Medical equipment repairers earned $35,340. Workers who assemble, adjust, and calibrate timing devices earned $22,420. For all types of instrumentation technicians, salaries ranged from $16,500 to $69,700.

Employee benefits vary but can include paid vacations and holidays, sick leave, insurance benefits, 401-K plans, profit sharing, pension plans, and tuition assistance programs.

Work Environment

Working conditions vary widely for instrumentation technicians. An oil refinery plant job is as different from space mission instrumentation work as a nuclear reactor instrumentation job is different from work in the surgical room of a hospital. All these jobs use similar principles, however, and instrumentation technicians can master new areas by applying what they have learned previously. For technicians who would like to travel, the petroleum industry, in particular, provides employment opportunities in foreign lands.

Instrumentation technicians' tasks may range from the routine to the highly complex and challenging. A calm, well-controlled approach to work is essential. Calibration and adjustment require the dexterity and control of a watchmaker. Consequently, a person who is easily excited or impatient is not well suited to this kind of employment.

Outlook

Employment opportunities for most instrumentation technicians will grow about as fast as the average through 2010. Opportunities will be best for graduates of postsecondary technical training programs. As technology becomes more sophisticated, employers will continue to look for technicians who are skilled in new technology and require a minimum of additional job training.

Most developments in automated manufacturing techniques, including robotics and computer-controlled machinery, rely heavily on instrumentation devices. The emerging fields of air and water pollution control are other areas of growth. Scientists and technicians measure the amount of toxic substances in the air or test water with the use of instrumentation.

Oceanography, including the search for undersea deposits of oil and minerals, is another expanding field for instrumentation technology, as is medical diagnosis, including long-distance diagnosis by physicians through the use of sensors, computers, and telephone lines.

One important field of growth is the teaching profession. As demand rises for skilled technicians, qualified instructors with combined knowledge of theory and application will be needed. Opportunities already exist, not only in educational institutions but also in those industries that have internal training programs.

For More Information

For information on educational programs and medical instrument certification, contact:
ASSOCIATION FOR THE ADVANCEMENT OF MEDICAL INSTRUMENTATION
1110 North Glebe Road, Suite 220
Arlington, VA 22201-4795
Tel: 800-332-2264
Email: certifications@aami.org
Web: http://www.aami.org

For information on careers and accreditation, contact:
INSTITUTE OF ELECTRICAL AND ELECTRONICS ENGINEERS, INC.
1828 L Street, NW, Suite 1202
Washington, DC 20036-5104
Tel: 202-785-0017
Web: http://www.ieee.org

For information on careers and student membership, contact:
**THE INSTRUMENTATION, SYSTEMS, AND AUTOMATION
SOCIETY**
67 Alexander Drive
Research Triangle Park, NC 27709
Tel: 919-549-8411
Email: info@isa.org
Web: http://www.isa.org

For information on careers and student clubs, contact:
JUNIOR ENGINEERING TECHNICAL SOCIETY
1420 King Street, Suite 405
Alexandria, VA 22314-2794
Tel: 703-548-5387
Email: jets@nae.edu
Web: http://www.jets.org

For information on certification, contact:
**NATIONAL INSTITUTE FOR CERTIFICATION IN ENGINEERING
TECHNOLOGIES**
1420 King Street
Alexandria, VA 22314-2794
Tel: 888-476-4238
Web: http://www.nicet.org

Marine Services Technicians

Overview

Marine services technicians inspect, maintain, and repair marine vessels, from small boats to large yachts. They work on vessels' hulls, engines, transmissions, navigational equipment, and electrical, propulsion, and refrigeration systems. Depending on their specialty, they may also be known as *motorboat mechanics, marine electronics technicians,* or *fiberglass technicians.* Marine services technicians may work at boat dealerships, boat repair shops, boat engine manufacturers, or marinas. Naturally, jobs are concentrated near large bodies of water and coastal areas.

Quick Facts

School Subjects
Mathematics
Technical/shop

Personal Skills
Following instructions
Mechanical/manipulative

Work Environment
Indoors and outdoors
One location with some travel

Minimum Education Level
Some postsecondary training

Salary Range
$17,320 to $26,660 to $41,490+

Certification or Licensing
Required for certain positions

Outlook
Little change or more slowly than the average

History

Ever since there have been boats and other water vessels, it has been necessary to have people who can repair and maintain them. In colonial times in the United States, those who took care of vessels were not called technicians, but they did many of the same routine tasks performed today, with less developed tools and equipment. They have had to keep up with developments in vessel design and material, from wood and iron to fiberglass.

In the past, those who repaired water vessels found work mainly with merchant boats and ships and with military vessels. As the wealth of the United States has grown, more people have been able to afford pleasure boats, from small motorcraft to luxury yachts. Marine services technicians rely on the pleasure boat industry today for much of their work.

The Job

Marine services technicians work on the more than 16 million boats and other watercraft owned by people in the United States. They test and repair boat engines, transmissions, and propellers; rigging, masts, and sails; and navigational equipment and steering gear. They repair or replace defective parts and sometimes make new parts to meet special needs. They may also inspect and replace internal cabinets, refrigeration systems, electrical systems and equipment, sanitation facilities, hardware, and trim.

Workers with specialized skills often have more specific titles. For example, *motorboat mechanics* work on boat engines—those that are inboard, outboard, and inboard/outboard. Routine maintenance tasks include lubricating, cleaning, repairing, and adjusting parts.

Motorboat mechanics often use special testing equipment, such as engine analyzers, compression gauges, ammeters, and voltmeters, as well as other computerized diagnostic equipment. Technicians must know how to disassemble and reassemble components and refer to service manuals for directions and specifications. Motorboat workers often install and repair electronics, sanitation, and air-conditioning systems. They need a set of general and specialized tools, often provided by their employers; many mechanics gradually acquire their own tools, often spending up to thousands of dollars on this investment.

Marine electronics technicians work with vessels' electronic safety and navigational equipment, such as radar, depth sounders, loran (long-range navigation), autopilots, and compass systems. They install, repair, and calibrate equipment for proper functioning. Routine maintenance tasks include checking, cleaning, repairing, and replacing parts. Electronics technicians check for common causes of problems, such as loose connections and defective parts. They often rely on schematics and manufacturers' specification manuals to troubleshoot problems. These workers also must have a set of tools, including hand tools such as pliers, screwdrivers, and soldering irons. Other equipment, often supplied by their employers, includes voltmeters, ohmmeters, signal generators, ammeters, and oscilloscopes.

Technicians who are *field repairers* go to the vessel to do their work, perhaps at the marina dock. *Bench repairers,* on the other hand, work on equipment brought into shops.

Some technicians work only on vessel hulls. These are usually made of either wood or fiberglass. *Fiberglass repairers* work on fiberglass hulls, of which most pleasure crafts today are built. They reinforce damaged areas of the hull, grind damaged pieces with a sander, or cut them away with a jigsaw and replace them using resin-impregnated fiberglass cloth. They finish the repaired sections by sanding, painting with a gel-coat substance, and then buffing.

Requirements

HIGH SCHOOL

Most employers prefer to hire applicants who have a high school diploma. If you are interested in this work, take mathematics classes and shop classes in metals, woodwork, and electronics while you are in high school. These classes will give you experience completing detailed and precise work. Shop classes will also give you experience using a variety of tools and reading blueprints. Take computer classes; you will probably be using this tool throughout your career for such things as diagnostic and design work. Science classes, such as physics, will also be beneficial to you. Finally, don't forget to take English classes. These classes will help you hone your reading and research skills, which will be needed when you consult technical manuals for repair and maintenance information throughout your career.

POSTSECONDARY TRAINING

Many marine services technicians learn their trade on the job. They find entry-level positions as general boatyard workers, doing such jobs as cleaning boat bottoms, and they work their way into the position of service technician. Or they may be hired as trainees. They learn how to perform typical service tasks under the supervision of experienced mechanics and gradually complete more difficult work. The training period may last for about three years.

Other technicians decide to get more formal training and attend vocational or technical colleges for classes in engine repair, electronics, and fiberglass work. Some schools, such as Northwest Technical College in Minnesota, Cape Fear Community College in North Carolina, and

Washington County Technical College in Maine, have programs specifically for marine technicians. These schools often offer an associate's degree in areas such as applied science. Classes students take may include mathematics, physics, electricity, schematic reading, and circuit theory. Boat manufacturers and other types of institutions, such as the American Boatbuilders and Repairers Association, the Mystic Seaport Museum, and the Wooden Boat School, offer skills training through less formal courses and seminars that often last several days or a few weeks. The military services can also provide training in electronics.

CERTIFICATION OR LICENSING

Those who test and repair marine radio transmitting equipment must have a general radio-telephone operator license from the Federal Communications Commission (1919 M Street, NW, Washington, DC 20554, Tel: 202-632-5050). Certification for technicians in the marine electronics industry is voluntary and is administered by the National Marine Electronics Association (see For More Information). There are three grades of Certified Marine Electronic Technicians: basic certification for technicians with one year of experience, advanced grade certification for those with three years of experience, and senior grade certification for those with 10 years of experience.

Basic certification is by written examination and the employer's verification as to the technician's proficiency in the repair of basic radar, depth sounders, and autopilots. The higher degrees of certification are earned by meeting all previous grade requirements plus satisfactorily completing a factory training course or having the employer attest to the technician's proficiency in repairing advanced equipment.

OTHER REQUIREMENTS

Most technicians work outdoors some of the time, and they are often required to test-drive the vessels they work on. This is considered an added benefit by many workers. Some workers in this field maintain that one of the most important qualities for a technician is a pleasant personality. Boat owners are often very proud of and attached to their vessels, so workers need to have both respect and authority when communicating with customers.

Technicians also need to be able to adapt to the cyclical nature of this business. They are often under a lot of pressure in the summer months, when most boat owners are enjoying the water and calling on technicians for service. On the other hand, they often have gaps in their work during the winter; some workers earn unemployment compensation at this time.

Motorboat technicians' work can sometimes be physically demanding, requiring them to lift heavy outboard motors or other components. Electronics technicians, on the other hand, must be able to work with delicate parts, such as wires and circuit boards; they should have good eyesight, color vision, and hearing (to listen for malfunctions revealed by sound).

Some marine services technicians may be required to provide their own hand tools. These tools are usually acquired over a period of time, but the collection may cost the mechanic hundreds if not thousands of dollars.

Exploring

This field lends itself to a lot of fun ways to explore job opportunities. Of course, having a boat of your own and working on it is one of the best means of preparation. If friends, neighbors, or relatives have boats, take trips with them and see how curious you are about what makes the vessel work. Offer to help do repairs to the boat, or at least watch while repairs are made and routine maintenance jobs are done. Clean up the deck, sand an old section of the hull, or polish the brass. If a boat just isn't available to you, try to find some type of engine to work on. Even working on an automobile engine will give you a taste of what this type of work is like.

Some high schools have co-op training programs through which students can look for positions with boat-related businesses, such as boat dealerships or even marinas. Check with your guidance counselor about this possibility. You also can read trade magazines such as *Boating Industry International* (http://boatbiz.com), *Professional Boatbuilder* (http://www.proboat.com), and *Marine Mechanics* (http://www.marinemechanics.com). These periodicals offer information monthly or bimonthly on the pleasure boat industry as well as on boat design, construction, and repair.

Employers

Marine services technicians are employed by boat retailers, boat repair shops, boat engine manufacturers, boat rental firms, resorts, and marinas. The largest marinas are in coastal areas, such as Florida, New York, California, Texas, Massachusetts, and Louisiana; smaller ones are located near lakes and water recreation facilities such as campgrounds. Manufacturers of large fishing vessels also employ technicians for on-site mechanical support at fishing sites and competitive events. These workers often follow professionals on the fishing circuit, traveling from tournament to tournament maintaining the vessels.

Starting Out

A large percentage of technicians get their start by working as general boatyard laborers—cleaning boats, cutting grass, painting, and so on. After showing interest and ability, they can begin to work with experienced technicians and learn skills on the job. Some professional organizations, such as the Marine Trades Association of New Jersey and the Michigan Boating Industries Association, offer scholarships for those interested in marine technician training.

For those technicians who have attended vocational or technical colleges, placement offices of these schools may have information about job openings.

Advancement

Many workers consider management and supervisory positions as job goals. After working for a number of years on actual repairs and maintenance, many technicians like to manage repair shops, supervise other workers, and deal with customers more directly. These positions require less physical labor but more communication and management skills. Many workers like to combine both aspects by becoming self-employed; they may have their own shops, attract their own jobs, and still get to do the technical work they enjoy.

Advancement often depends on an individual's interests. Some become marina managers, manufacturers' salespersons, or field representatives. Others take a different direction and work as *boat brokers*, selling boats. *Marine surveyors* verify the condition and value of boats; they are independent contractors hired by insurance companies and lending institutions such as banks.

Earnings

According to the U.S. Department of Labor, the median yearly earnings of motorboat mechanics were $26,660 in 2000. The middle 50 percent earned between $20,760 and $33,680. Salaries ranged from less than $17,320 to more than $41,490 a year. Median annual earnings of boat dealers, the industry employing the largest numbers of motorboat mechanics, were $26,350. The *O*Net Dictionary of Occupational Titles* reported a yearly income of $27,612 for the field of marine services technicians.

Technicians in small shops tend to receive few fringe benefits, but larger employers often offer paid vacations, sick leave, and health insurance. Some employers provide uniforms and tools and pay for work-related training. Many technicians who enjoy the hands-on work with boats claim that the best benefit is being able to perform a craft they enjoy and to take repaired boats out for test drives.

Work Environment

Technicians who work indoors often are in well-lit and ventilated shops. The work is cleaner than that on cars because there tends to be less grease and dirt on marine engines; instead, workers have to deal with water scum, heavy-duty paint, and fiberglass. In general, marine work is similar to other types of mechanical jobs, where workers encounter such things as noise when engines are being run and potential danger with power tools and chemicals. Also similar to other mechanics' work, sometimes technicians work alone on a job, and at other times they work on a boat with other technicians. Unless a technician is self-employed, his or her work will likely be overseen by a supervisor of some kind. For any repair job, the technician may have to deal directly with customers.

Some mechanics, such as those who work at marinas, work primarily outdoors—and in all kinds of weather. In boats with no air conditioning, the conditions in the summer can be hot and uncomfortable. Technicians often have to work in tight, uncomfortable places to perform repairs. Sailboats have especially tight access to inboard engines.

There is often a big demand for service just before Memorial Day and the Fourth of July. In the summer, workweeks can average 60 hours, whereas in winter, the week can involve less than 40 hours of work, with layoffs common at this time of year. In the warmer climates of the United States, work tends to be steadier throughout the year.

Outlook

According to the U.S. Department of Labor, employment opportunities for small engine mechanics, including marine services technicians, are expected to grow more slowly than the average through 2010. As boat design and construction become more complicated, the outlook will be best for well-trained technicians. Most marine craft purchases are made by the over-40 age group, which is expected to increase over the next decade. The growth of this population segment should help expand the market for motorboats and increase the demand for qualified mechanics.

The availability of jobs will be related to the health of the pleasure boat industry. According to *Boating Industry*, there are 10,000 marine retailers in the United States and 1,500 boatyards that repair hulls and engines. One interesting demographic trend that will influence job opportunities is the shift of the population to the South and West, where warm-weather seasons are longer and thus attract more boating activity.

An increase in foreign demand for U.S. pleasure vessels will mean more opportunities for workers in this field. U.S. manufacturers are expected to continue to develop foreign markets and establish more distribution channels. However, legislation in the United States may require boat operator licenses and stricter emission standards, which might lead to a decrease in the number of boats sold and maintained here.

For More Information

To find out whether there is a marine association in your area, contact:
MARINE RETAIL ASSOCIATION OF AMERICA
150 East Huron Street, Suite 802
Chicago, IL 60611
Email: mraa@mraa.com
Web: http://www.mraa.com

For information on certification, the industry, and membership, contact:
NATIONAL MARINE ELECTRONICS ASSOCIATION
7 Riggs Avenue
Severna Park, MD 21146
Email: info@nmea.org
Web: http://www.nmea.org

For educational information, contact the following:

CAPE FEAR COMMUNITY COLLEGE
411 North Front Street
Wilmington, NC 28401-3993
Tel: 910-362-7000
Web: http://cfcc.net

NORTHWEST TECHNICAL COLLEGE
Tel: 877-SEEK-NTC
Email: info@mail.ntc.mnscu.edu
Web: http://www.ntcmn.edu

WASHINGTON COUNTY TECHNICAL COLLEGE
Eastport Campus
16 Deep Cove Road
Eastport, ME 04631
Tel: 800-806-0433
Email: admissions@wctc.org
Web: http://www.wctc.org

Musical Instrument Repairers and Tuners

Overview

Musical instrument repairers and tuners work on a variety of instruments, often operating inside music shops or repair shops to keep the pieces in tune and in proper condition. Those who specialize in working on pianos or pipe organs may travel to the instrument's location to work. Instrument repairers and tuners usually specialize in certain families of musical instruments, such as stringed or brass instruments. Depending on the instrument, they may be skilled in working with wood, metal, electronics, or other materials. There are approximately 8,000 musical instrument repairers and tuners employed in the United States.

History

The world's first musical instrument was the human body. Paleolithic dancers clapped, stamped, chanted, and slapped their bodies to mark rhythm. Gourd rattles, bone whistles, scrapers, hollow branch and conch shell trumpets, wooden rhythm pounders and knockers, and bullroarers followed. By the early Neolithic times, people had developed drums that produced two or more pitches and pottery and cane flutes that gave several notes. The musical bow, a primitive stringed instrument and forerunner of the jaw harp, preceded the bow-shaped harp (about 3000 BC) and the long-necked lute (about 2000 BC).

The history of the pipe organ stretches back to the third century BC, when the Egyptians developed an organ that used water power to produce a stream of air. A few centuries later, organs appeared in Byzantium that used bellows (a device that draws air in and then expels it with great force) to send air through the organ pipes. From that time until about AD 1500 all the features of the modern pipe organ were developed.

The first version of the violin, played by scraping a taut bow across several stretched strings, appeared in Europe around the year 1510. The end of the 16th century saw the development of the violin as it is known today. Over the next hundred years, violin making reached its greatest achievements in the area around Cremona, Italy, where families of master craftsmen, such as the Stradivaris, the Guarneris, and the Amatis, set a standard for quality that never has been surpassed. Today, their violins are coveted by players around the world for their tonal quality.

The modern piano is the end product of a gradual evolution from plucked string instruments, such as the harp, to instruments employing hammers of one kind or another to produce notes by striking the strings. By the late 1700s, the immediate ancestor of the modern piano had been developed. Improvements and modifications (most involving new materials or manufacturing processes) took place throughout the 19th century, resulting in today's piano.

In addition to the stringed instruments, contemporary orchestral instruments also include the woodwind, brass, and percussion families. Woodwinds include the flute, clarinet, oboe, bassoon, and saxophone. Brass instruments include the French horn, trumpet, cornet, trombone, and tuba. All require some professional care and maintenance at some time. The modern electronic organ is a descendant of the pipe organ. In 1934, Laurens Hammond, an American inventor, patented the first practical electronic organ, an instrument that imitates the sound of the pipe organ but requires much less space and is more economical and practical to own and operate. The development of electronic and computer technology produced the first synthesizers and synthesized instruments, which are used widely today.

The Job

All but the most heavily damaged instruments usually can be repaired by competent, experienced craft workers. In addition, instruments require regular maintenance and inspection to ensure that they play properly and to prevent small problems from becoming major ones.

Stringed-instrument repairers perform extremely detailed and difficult work. The repair of violins, violas, and cellos might be considered the finest woodworking done in the world today. Because their sound quality is so beautiful, some older, rarer violins are worth millions of dollars, and musicians will sometimes fly halfway around the world to have rare instruments repaired by master restorers. In many ways, the work of these master craftspeople may be compared to the restoration of fine art masterpieces.

When a violin or other valuable stringed instrument needs repair, its owner takes the instrument to a repair shop, which may employ many repairers. If the violin has cracks in its body, it must be taken apart. The pieces of a violin are held together by a special glue that allows the instrument to be dismantled easily for repair purposes. The glue, which is made from hides and bones and has been used for more than 400 years, is sturdy but does not bond permanently with the wood.

To repair a crack in the back of a violin, the repairer first pops the back off the instrument. After cleaning the crack with warm water, the repairer glues the crack and attaches cleats or studs above the crack on the inside to prevent further splitting. The repairer reassembles the violin and closes the outside of the crack with fill varnish. Lastly, the repairer treats the crack scrupulously with retouch varnish so that it becomes invisible.

The repairer does not complete every step immediately after the previous one. Depending on the age and value of the instrument, a repair job can take three weeks or longer. Glues and varnishes need to set, and highly detailed work demands much concentration. The repairer also needs to do research to isolate the original type of varnish on the instrument and match it precisely with modern materials. The repairer usually has more than one repair job going at any one time.

A major restoration, such as the replacement of old patchwork or the fitting of inside patches to support the instrument, requires even more time. A large project can take two years or longer. A master restorer can put 2,000 or more hours into the repair of a valuable violin that has nothing more than a few cracks in its finish. Since many fine instruments are worth $2,000,000 or more, they need intense work to preserve the superior quality of their sound. The repairer cannot rush the work, must concentrate on every detail, and must complete the repair properly or risk other problems later on.

While all instruments are not made by Stradivari, they still need to be kept in good condition to be played well. Owners bring in their violins, violas, and cellos to the repair shop every season for cleaning, inspecting joints, and gluing gaps. The work involves tools similar to woodworker's tools, such as carving knives, planes, and gouges. The violin repairer will often need to play the instrument to check its condition and tune it. Bow rehairers maintain the quality of the taut, vibrating horsehair string that is stretched from end to end of the resilient wooden bow.

Wind-instrument repairers require a similar level of skill to that required of stringed-instrument repairers. However, as the quality of sound is more standard among manufacturers, old instruments do not necessarily play any better than new ones, and these instruments do not command the same value as a fine violin.

The repairer first needs to determine the extent of repairs that the instrument warrants. The process may range from a few minor repairs to bring the instrument up to playing condition to a complete overhaul. After fixing the instrument, the repairer also will clean both the inside and outside and may replate the metal finish on a scuffed or rusty instrument.

For woodwinds such as clarinets and oboes, common repairs include fixing or replacing the moving parts of the instrument, including replacing broken keys with new keys, cutting new padding or corks to replace worn pieces, and replacing springs. If the body of the woodwind is cracked in any sections, the repairer will take the instrument apart and attempt to pin or glue the crack shut. In some situations, the repairer will replace the entire section or joint of the instrument.

Repairing brass instruments such as trumpets and French horns requires skill in metalworking and plating. The pieces of these instruments are held together by solder, which the repairer must heat and remove to take the instrument apart for repair work. To fix dents, the repairer will unsolder the piece and work the dent out with hammers and more delicate tools and seal splits in the metal with solder as well. A final buffing and polishing usually removes any evidence of the repair.

If one of the valves of the brass instrument is leaking, the repairer may replate it and build up layers of metal to fill the gaps. At times, the repairer will replace a badly damaged valve with a new valve from the instrument manufacturer, but often the owner will discard the entire instrument because the cost of making a new valve from raw materials is prohibitive. Replacement parts are usually available from the manufacturer, but parts for older instruments are sometimes difficult or impossible to find. For this reason, many repairers save and stockpile discarded instruments for their parts.

Piano technicians and *piano tuners* repair and tune pianos so that when a key is struck it will produce its correctly pitched note of the musical scale. A piano may go out of tune for a variety of reasons, including strings that have stretched or tightened from age, temperature change, relocation, or prolonged use. Tuners use a special wrench to adjust the pins that control the tension on the strings. Piano tuners usually are specially trained for such work, but piano technicians also may perform tuning in connection with a more thorough inspection or overhaul of an instrument.

A piano's performance is also affected by problems in any of the thousands of moving parts of the action or by problems in the sounding board or the frame holding the strings. These are problems that the technician is trained to analyze and correct. They may involve replacing or repairing parts or making adjustments that enable the existing parts to function more smoothly.

The life of a piano—that is, the period of time before it can no longer be properly tuned or adjusted to correct operational problems— is usually estimated at 20 years. Because the harp and strong outer wooden frame are seldom damaged, technicians often rebuild pianos by replacing the sounding board and strings, refurbishing and replacing parts where necessary, and refinishing the outer case.

In all their work, from tuning to rebuilding, piano technicians discover a piano's problems by talking to the owner and playing the instrument themselves. They may dismantle a piano partially on-site to determine the amount of wear to its parts and look for broken parts. They use common hand tools such as hammers, screwdrivers, and pliers. To repair and rebuild pianos, they use a variety of specialized tools for stringing and setting pins.

For *pipe organ technicians*, the largest part of the job is repairing and maintaining existing organs. This primarily involves tuning the pipes, which can be time consuming, even in a moderate-sized organ.

To tune a flue pipe, the technician moves a slide that increases or decreases the length of the speaking (note-producing) part of the pipe, varying its pitch. The technician tunes a reed pipe by varying the length of the brass reed inside the pipe.

To tune an organ, the technician tunes either the A or C pipes by matching their notes with those of a tuning fork or electronic note-producing device. He or she then tunes the other pipes in harmony with the A or C notes. This may require a day or more for a moderate-sized organ and much longer for a giant concert organ.

Pipe organ technicians also diagnose, locate, and correct problems in the operating parts of the organ and perform preventive maintenance on a regular basis. To do this, they work with electric wind-generating equipment and with slides, valves, keys, air channels, and other equipment that enables the organist to produce the desired music.

Occasionally, a new organ is installed in a new or existing structure. Manufacturers design and install the largest organs. Each is unique, and the designer carefully supervises its construction and installation. Often, designers individually create moderate-sized organs specifically for the structures, usually churches, in which they will be played. Technicians follow the designer's blueprints closely during installation. The work involves assembling and connecting premanufactured components using a variety of hand and power tools. Technicians may work in teams, especially when installing the largest pipes of the organ.

Although the electronic organ imitates the sound of the pipe organ, the workings of the two instruments have little in common. The electronic organ consists of electrical and electronic components and circuits that channel electrical current through various oscillators and amplifiers to produce sound when a player presses each key. It is rare for an oscillator or other component to need adjustment in the way an organ pipe needs to be adjusted to tune it. A technician tunes an electronic organ by testing it for electronic malfunction and replacing or repairing the component, circuit board, or wire.

The work of the *electronic organ technician* is closer to that of the television repair technician than it is to that of the pipe organ technician. The technician often begins looking for the source of a problem by checking for loose wires and solder connections. After making routine checks, technicians consult wiring diagrams that enable them to trace and test the circuits of the entire instrument to find malfunctions. For instance, an unusual or irregular voltage in a circuit may indicate a problem. Once the problem has been located, the technician often solves it by replacing a malfunctioning part, such as a circuit board.

These technicians work with common electrician's tools: pliers, wire cutters, screwdrivers, soldering irons, and testing equipment. Technicians can make most repairs and adjustments in the customer's home. Because each manufacturer's instruments are arranged differently, technicians follow manufacturers' wiring diagrams and service manuals to locate trouble spots and make repairs. In larger and more complex instruments, such as those in churches and theaters, this may require a day or more of searching and testing.

Other types of repairers work on a variety of less common instruments. *Percussion tuners and repairers* work on drums, bells, congas, timbales, cymbals, and castanets. They may stretch new skins over the instrument, replace broken or missing parts, or seal cracks in the wood.

Accordion tuners and repairers work on free-reed portable accordions, piano accordions, concertinas, harmoniums, and harmonicas. They repair leaks in the bellows of an instrument, replace broken or damaged reeds, and perform various maintenance tasks. Other specialists in instrument repair include fretted-instrument repairers, harp regulators, trombone-slide assemblers, metal-reed tuners, tone regulators, and chip tuners.

In addition to repair work, those who run their own music or repair shops perform duties similar to others in the retail business. They order stock from instrument manufacturers, wait on customers, handle their accounting and billing work, and perform other duties.

Requirements

HIGH SCHOOL

No matter what family of instruments interests you, you should start preparing for this field by gaining a basic knowledge of music. Take high school classes in music history, music theory, and choir, chorus, or other singing classes. By learning to read music, developing an ear for scales, and understanding tones and pitches, you will be developing an excellent background for this work. Also, explore your interest in instruments (besides your own voice) by taking band or orchestra classes or private music lessons. By learning how to play an instrument, you will also learn how a properly tuned and maintained instrument should sound. If you find yourself interested in instruments with metal parts, consider taking art or shop classes that provide the opportunity to do metalworking. These classes will allow you to practice soldering and work with appropriate tools. If you are interested in piano or stringed instruments, consider taking art or shop classes that offer woodworking. In these classes you will learn finishing techniques and use tools that you may relate to the building and maintaining of the bodies of these instruments.

Because instrument repair of any type is precision work, you will benefit from taking mathematics classes such as algebra and geometry. Since many instrument repairers and tuners are self-employed, take business or accounting classes to prepare for this possibility. Finally, take English classes to develop your research, reading, and communication skills. You will often need to consult technical instruction manuals for repair and maintenance work. You will also need strong communication skills that will help you broaden your client base as well as help you explain to your clients what work needs to be done.

POSTSECONDARY TRAINING

There are two main routes to becoming a music instrument repairer and tuner: extensive apprenticeship or formal education through technical or vocational schools. Apprenticeships, however, can be difficult to find. You will simply need to contact instrument repair shops and request a position as a trainee. Once you have found a position, the training period may last from two to five years. You will get hands-on experience working with the instruments as well as having other duties around the shop, such as selling any products offered.

Depending on the family of instruments you want to work with, there are a number of technical or vocational schools that offer either courses or full-time programs in repair and maintenance work. Professional organizations may have information on such schools. The National Association of Professional Band Instrument Repair Technicians, for example, provides a listing of schools offering programs in band instrument repair. The Piano Technicians Guild has information on both full-time programs and correspondence courses. Wind-instrument repairers can learn their craft at one of the handful of vocational schools in the country that offers classes in instrument repair. Entrance requirements vary among schools, but all require at least a high school diploma or GED. Typical classes that are part of any type of instrument repair and tuning education include acoustics, tool care and operation, and small business practices. Depending on what instrument you choose to specialize in, you may also study topics such as buffing, dent removal, plating, soldering, or woodworking. You may also be required to invest in personal hand tools and supplies, and you may need to make tools that are not available from suppliers.

If you are interested in working with electronic organs, you will need at least one year of electronics technical training to learn organ repair skills. Electronics training is available from community colleges and technical and vocational schools. The U.S. Armed Forces also offer excellent training in electronics, which you can apply to instrument work. Electronic organ technicians also may attend training courses offered by electronic organ manufacturers.

It is important to keep in mind that even those who take courses or attend school for their postsecondary training will need to spend years honing their skills.

A number of instrument repairers and tuners have completed some college work or have a bachelor's degree. A 1997 Piano Technicians Guild survey (the most recent statistics available), for example, shows that at least 50 percent of the Guild's members had bachelor's degrees or higher. Although there are no college degrees in instrument repair, people who major in some type of music performance may find that this background adds to their understanding of the work.

CERTIFICATION OR LICENSING

The Piano Technicians Guild helps its members improve their skills and keep up with developments in piano technology. Refresher courses and seminars in new developments are offered by local chapters, and courses offered by manufacturers are publicized in Guild publications. The Guild also administers a series of tests that can lead to certification as a Registered Piano Technician.

OTHER REQUIREMENTS

Personal qualifications for people in this occupational group include keen hearing and eyesight, mechanical aptitude, and manual dexterity. They should be resourceful and able to learn on the job because every instrument that needs repair is unique and requires individual care. Instrument repairers and tuners must also have the desire to learn throughout their professional lives. They expand their knowledge by studying trade magazines and manufacturers' service manuals related to new developments in their field. They may improve their skills in training programs and at regional and national seminars. Instrument manufacturers often offer training in the repair of their particular products.

Other qualifications for the instrument repairer and tuner are related to his or her instrument specialty. For example, the majority of piano technicians work in customers' homes, and they should be able to communicate clearly when talking about a piano's problems and when advising a customer. A pleasant manner and good appearance are important to instill confidence. While the physical strength required for moving a piano is not often needed, the technician may be required to bend or stand in awkward positions while working on the piano. Those interested in careers as pipe organ technicians need the ability to follow blueprints and printed instructions to plan and execute repair or installation work. And any repairer and tuner who works in a store selling musical instruments should be comfortable working with the public.

Exploring

One of the best ways to explore this field is to take some type of musical instrument lessons. This experience will help you develop an ear for tonal quality and acquaint you with the care of your instrument. It will also put you in contact with those who work professionally with music. You may develop a contact with someone at the store where you have purchased or rented your instrument, and, naturally, you will get to know your music teacher. Ask these people what they know about the repair and tuning business. Your high school or local college music departments can also be excellent places for meeting those who work with instruments. Ask teachers in these departments whom they know working in instrument repair. You may be able to set up an informational interview with a repairer and tuner you find through these contacts. Ask the repairer about his or her education, how he or she got interested in the work, what he or she would recommend for someone considering the field, and any other questions you may have.

Part-time and summer jobs that are related closely to this occupation may be difficult to obtain because full-time trainees usually handle the routine tasks of a helper. Nevertheless, it is worth applying for such work at music stores and repair shops in case they do not use full-time trainees. General clerical jobs in stores that sell musical instruments may help familiarize you with the language of the field and may offer you the opportunity to observe skilled repairers at work.

Employers

Approximately 8,000 people work as musical instrument repairers and tuners of all types in the United States. About one-fourth of this number are self-employed and may operate out of their own homes. The majority of the rest work in repair shops and music stores and for manufacturers. Large cities with extensive professional music activity, both in the United States and in Europe, are the best places of employment.

Musical centers such as Chicago, New York, London, and Vienna are the hubs of the repair business for stringed instruments, and any repairer who wishes a sufficient amount of work may have to relocate to one of these cities.

Some piano technicians work in factories where pianos are made. They may assemble and adjust pianos or inspect the finished instruments. Some technicians work in shops that rebuild pianos. Many piano repairers and tuners work in customers' homes.

Most of the few hundred pipe organ technicians in the United States are self-employed. These pipe organ technicians are primarily engaged in repairing and tuning existing organs. A small number are employed by organ manufacturers and are engaged in testing and installing new instruments. The great expense involved in manufacturing and installing a completely new pipe organ decreases demand and makes this type of work scarce.

Starting Out

Vocational schools and community colleges that offer instrument repair training can usually connect recent graduates with repair shops that have job openings. Those who enter the field through apprenticeships work at the local shop where they are receiving their training. Professional organizations may also have information on job openings.

Advancement

Repairers and tuners may advance their skills by participating in special training programs. A few who work for large dealers or repair shops may move into supervisory positions.

Another path to advancement is to open one's own musical repair shop and service. Before doing this, however, the worker should have adequate training to survive the strong competition that exists in the tuning and repair business. In many cases, repairers may need to continue working for another employer until they develop a clientele large enough to support a full-time business.

A few restorers of stringed instruments earn worldwide reputations for their exceptional skill. Their earnings and the caliber of their customers both rise significantly when they become well known. It takes a great deal of hard work and talent to achieve such professional standing, however, and this recognition comes only after years in the field. At any one time, there may be perhaps 10 restorers in the world who perform exceptional work, while another hundred or so are known for doing very good work. The work of these few craftspeople is always in great demand.

Earnings

Wages vary depending on geographic area and the worker's specialty and skill. Full-time instrument repairers and tuners had a median income of about $31,408 in 2000, according to the U.S. Department of Labor. The highest-paid 10 percent earned $65,458 or more per year. Some helpers work for the training they get and receive no pay. Repairers and tuners who are self-employed earn more than those who work for music stores or instrument manufacturers, but their income is generally less stable. Repairers who gain an international reputation for the quality of their work earn the highest income in this field.

Repairers and tuners working as employees of manufacturers or stores often receive some benefits, including health insurance, vacation days, and holiday and sick pay. Self-employed repairers and tuners must provide these benefits for themselves.

Work Environment

Repairers and tuners work in shops, homes, and instrument factories, surrounded by the tools and materials of their trade. The atmosphere is somewhat quiet, but the pace is often busy. Since repairers and tuners are usually paid by the piece, they have to concentrate and work diligently on their repairs. Piano technicians and tuners generally perform their work in homes, schools, churches, and other places where pianos are located.

Instrument tuners and repairers may work more than 40 hours a week, especially during the fall and winter, when people spend more time indoors playing musical instruments. Self-employed tuners and repairers often work evenings and weekends, when it is more convenient to meet with the customer.

As noted, many repairs demand extreme care and often long periods of time to complete. For large instruments, such as pianos and pipe organs, repairers and tuners may have to work in cramped locations for some length of time, bending, stretching, and using tools that require physical strength to handle. Tuning pianos and organs often requires many hours and can be tedious work.

The field at times may be very competitive, especially among the more prestigious repair shops for stringed instruments. Most people at the major repair shops know each other and vie for the same business. There is often a great deal of pressure from owners to fix their instruments as soon as possible, but a conscientious repairer cannot be rushed into doing a mediocre job. In spite of these drawbacks, repair work is almost always interesting, challenging, and rewarding. Repairers never do the same job twice, and each instrument comes with its own set of challenges. The work requires repairers to call on their ingenuity, skill, and personal pride every day.

Outlook

Job opportunities for musical instrument repairers and tuners are expected to grow more slowly than the average through 2010, according to the U.S. Department of Labor. This is a small, specialized field, and replacement needs will be the source of most jobs. Because training positions and school programs are relatively difficult to find, those with thorough training and education will have the best employment outlook.

It is a luxury for most owners to have their instruments tuned and repaired, and they tend to postpone these services when money is scarce. Tuners and repairers therefore may lose income during economic downturns. In addition, few trainees are hired at repair shops or music stores when business is slow.

For More Information

For information on organ and choral music fields, contact:
AMERICAN GUILD OF ORGANISTS/*THE AMERICAN ORGANIST MAGAZINE*
475 Riverside Drive, Suite 1260
New York, NY 10115
Tel: 212-870-2310
Email: info@agohq.org
Web: http://www.agohq.org

For information about electronic instrument repair, contact:
ELECTRONIC INDUSTRIES ALLIANCE
2500 Wilson Boulevard
Arlington, VA 22201
Tel: 703-907-7790
Web: http://www.eia.org

ELECTRONICS TECHNICIANS ASSOCIATION
5 Depot Street
Greencastle, IN 46135
Tel: 800-288-3824
Email: eta@tds.net
Web: http://eta-sda.com

For information about instrument repair and a list of schools offering courses in the field, contact:
NATIONAL ASSOCIATION OF PROFESSIONAL BAND INSTRUMENT REPAIR TECHNICIANS, INC.
PO Box 51
Normal, IL 61761
Tel: 309-452-4257
Email: chagler@napbirt.org
Web: http://www.napbirt.org

For information on certification, contact:
PIANO TECHNICIANS GUILD
3930 Washington
Kansas City, MO 64111-2963
Tel: 816-753-7747
Email: ptg@ptg.org
Web: http://www.ptg.org

Packaging Machinery Technicians

Quick Facts

School Subjects
 Mathematics
 Technical/shop
Personal Skills
 Mechanical/manipulative
 Technical/scientific
Work Environment
 Primarily indoors
 Primarily multiple locations
Minimum Education Level
 High school diploma
Salary Range
 $13,250 to $46,976 to $70,000
Certification or Licensing
 Voluntary
Outlook
 Faster than the average

Overview

Packaging machinery technicians work with automated machinery that packages products into bottles, cans, bags, boxes, cartons, and other containers. The machines perform various operations, such as forming, filling, closing, labeling, and marking. The systems and technologies that packaging machinery technicians work with are diverse. Depending on the job, packaging machinery technicians may work with electrical, mechanical, hydraulic, or pneumatic systems. They also may work with computerized controllers, fiber-optic transmitters, robotic units, and vision systems.

History

Packaging has been used since ancient times when people first wrapped food in materials to protect it or devised special carriers to transport items over long distances. One of the oldest packaging materials, glass, was used by Egyptians as early as 3000 BC. Packaging as we know it, though, has its origins in the Industrial Revolution. Machinery was used for mass production of items, and manufacturers needed some way to package products and protect them during transport. Packages and containers were developed that not only kept goods from damage during shipment but also helped to increase the shelf life of perishable items.

Initially, packaging was done by hand. Workers at manufacturing plants hand-packed products into paper boxes, steel cans, glass jars, or other containers as they were produced. As manufacturing processes and methods improved, equipment and machines were developed to provide quicker and less expensive ways to package products. Automated machinery was in use by the 19th century and was used not only to package products but also to create packaging materials. The first containers produced through automated machinery were glass containers created by Michael Owens in Toledo, Ohio, in 1903.

The use of new packaging materials, such as cellophane in the 1920s and aluminum cans in the early 1960s, required updated machinery to handle the new materials and to provide faster, more efficient production. Semiautomatic machines and eventually high-speed, fully automated machines were created to handle a wide variety of products, materials, and packaging operations. Today, packaging engineers, packaging machinery technicians, and other engineering professionals work to develop new equipment and techniques that are more time-, material-, and cost-efficient. Advanced technologies, such as robotics, are allowing for the creation of increasingly sophisticated packaging machinery.

The Job

Packaging machinery technicians work in packaging plants of various industries or in the plants of packaging machinery manufacturers. Their jobs entail building machines, installing and setting up equipment, training operators to use the equipment, maintaining equipment, troubleshooting, and repairing machines. Many of the machines today are computer-controlled and may include robotic or vision-guided applications.

Machinery builders, also called *assemblers,* assist engineers in the development and modification of new and existing machinery designs. They build different types of packaging machinery following engineering blueprints, wiring schematics, pneumatic diagrams, and plant layouts. Beginning with a machine frame that has been welded in another department, they assemble electrical circuitry, mechanical components, and fabricated items that they may have made themselves in the plant's machine shop. They may also be responsible for bolting on additional elements of the machine to the frame. After the machinery is assembled, they perform a test run to make sure it is performing according to specifications.

Field service technicians, also called *field service representatives,* are employed by packaging machinery manufacturers. They do most of their work at the plants where the packaging machinery is being used. In some companies, assemblers may serve as field service technicians; in others, the field service representative is a technician other than the assembler. In either case, they install new machinery at customers' plants and train in-plant machine operators and maintenance personnel on its operation and maintenance.

When a new machine is delivered, the field service technicians level it and anchor it to the plant floor. Then, following engineering drawings, wiring plans, and plant layouts, they install the system's electrical and electromechanical components. They also regulate the controls and setup for the size, thickness, and type of material to be processed and ensure the correct sequence of processing stages. After installation, the technicians test-run the machinery and make any necessary adjustments. Then they teach machine operators the proper operating and maintenance procedures for that piece of equipment. The entire installation process, which may take a week, is carefully documented. Field service representatives may also help the plant's in-house mechanics troubleshoot equipment already in operation, including modifying equipment for greater efficiency and safety.

Automated packaging machine mechanics, also called *maintenance technicians,* perform scheduled preventive maintenance as well as diagnose machinery problems and make repairs. Preventive maintenance is done on a regular basis following the manufacturer's guidelines in the service manual. During routine maintenance, technicians change filters in vacuum pumps, grease fittings, change oil in gearboxes, and replace worn bushings, chains, and belts. When machines do break down, maintenance technicians must work quickly to fix them so that production can resume as soon as possible. The technician might be responsible for all the machinery in the plant, one or more packaging lines, or a single machine. In a small plant, a single technician may be responsible for all the duties required to keep a packaging line running, while in a large plant a team of technicians may divide the duties.

Requirements

HIGH SCHOOL
Although a high school diploma is not required, it is preferred by most employers who hire packaging or engineering technicians. In high school, you should take geometry and voc-tech classes such as electri-

cal shop, machine shop, and mechanical drawing. Computer classes, including computer-aided design, are also helpful. In addition to developing mechanical and electrical abilities, you should develop communication skills through English and writing classes.

POSTSECONDARY TRAINING

Many employers prefer to hire technicians who have completed a two-year technical training program. Completing a machinery training program or packaging machinery program can provide you with the necessary knowledge and technical skills for this type of work. Machinery training programs are available at community colleges, trade schools, and technical institutes throughout the country, but there are only a few technical colleges specializing in packaging machinery programs. These programs award either a degree or certificate in automated packaging machinery systems. You may get a list of these technical colleges by writing to the Packaging Machinery Manufacturers Institute.

Packaging machinery programs generally last two years and include extensive hands-on training as well as classroom study. You learn to use simple hand tools, such as hacksaws, drill presses, lathes, mills, and grinders. Other technical courses cover sheet metal and welding work, power transmission, electrical and mechanical systems, maintenance operations, industrial safety, and hazardous materials handling.

Classes in packaging operations include bag making, loading, and closing; case loading; blister packaging; palletizing, conveying, and accumulating; and labeling and bar coding. There are also classes in form fill, seal wrap, and carton machines as well as packaging quality control and package design and testing. Courses especially critical in an industry where technology is increasingly sophisticated are PLC (programmable logic control), CAD/CAM (computer-aided design and manufacturing), fiber optics, robotics, and servo controls.

CERTIFICATION OR LICENSING

Although employers may not require certification, it can provide a competitive advantage when seeking employment. A voluntary certification program is available for engineering technicians through the National Institute for Certification in Engineering Technologies. Certification is available at various levels and in different specialty fields. Most programs require passing a written exam and possessing a certain amount of work experience. The Institute of Packaging Professionals offers the following voluntary certifications: Certified Professional in Training (professionals with less than six years of experience in packaging) and Certified Packaging Professional (professionals with at least six years of experience in packaging).

Union membership may be a requirement for some jobs, depending on union activity at a particular company. Unions are more likely found in large-scale national and international corporations. Field service technicians are usually not unionized. Maintenance technicians and assemblers may be organized by the International Brotherhood of Teamsters or the International Association of Machinists and Aerospace Workers. In addition, some technicians may be represented by the International Longshoremen's and Warehousemen's Union.

OTHER REQUIREMENTS

Persons interested in this field should have mechanical and electrical aptitudes, manual dexterity, and the ability to work under time pressure. In addition, they should have analytical and problem-solving skills. The ability to communicate effectively with people from varying backgrounds is especially important, as packaging machinery technicians work closely with engineers, plant managers, customers, and machinery operators. They need to be able to listen to workers' problems as well as to explain things clearly. They frequently have to provide written reports, so good writing skills are beneficial.

Exploring

You can test your interest in this type of work by engaging in activities that require mechanical and electrical skills, such as building a short-wave radio, taking appliances apart, and working on cars, motorcycles, and bicycles. Participating in science clubs and contests can also provide opportunities for working with electrical and mechanical equipment and building and repairing things. Taking vocational shop classes can also help you explore your interests and acquire useful skills.

Employers

Packaging machinery technicians are usually employed by companies that manufacture packaging machinery or by companies that package the products they produce. Packaging is one of the largest industries in the United States, so jobs are plentiful across the country, in small towns and large cities. Opportunities in the packaging field can be found in almost any company that produces and packages a product. Food, chemicals, cosmetics, electronics, pharmaceuticals, automotive parts, hardware, plastics, and almost any products you can think of need to be packaged before reaching the consumer market. Because of this diversity, jobs are not restricted to any product, geographic location, or plant size.

Starting Out

If you are enrolled in a technical program, you may find job leads through your school's job placement service. Many jobs in packaging are unadvertised—you find out about them only through contacts with professionals in the industry. You can also learn about openings from teachers, school administrators, and industry contacts acquired during training.

You can apply directly to machinery manufacturing companies or companies with manufacturing departments. Local employment offices may list job openings. Sometimes companies hire part-time or summer help in other departments, such as the warehouse or shipping. These jobs may provide an opportunity to move into other areas of the company.

Advancement

Technicians usually begin in entry-level positions and work as part of an engineering team. They may advance from a maintenance technician to an assembler and then move up to a supervisory position in production operations or packaging machinery. They can also become project managers and field service managers.

Workers who show an interest in their work, learn quickly, and have good technical skills can gradually take on more responsibilities and advance to higher positions. The ability to work as part of a team and communicate well with others, self-motivation, and the ability to work well without a lot of supervision are all helpful traits for advancement. People who have skills as a packaging machinery technician can usually transfer those skills to engineering technician positions in other industries.

Some packaging machinery technicians pursue additional education to qualify as an engineer and move into electrical engineering, mechanical engineering, packaging engineering, or industrial engineering positions. Other technicians pursue business, economics, and finance degrees and use these credentials to obtain positions in other areas of the manufacturing process, in business development, or in areas such as importing or exporting.

Earnings

In general, technicians earn approximately $20,000 a year to start and with experience can increase their salaries to about $33,000. Seasoned workers with two-year degrees who work for large companies may earn between $50,000 and $70,000 a year, particularly those in field service jobs or supervisory positions.

According to Abbott-Langer Associates, packaging equipment operators in the food industry earned an average of $28,288 a year in 2000. Machine repairers earned an average of $30,472. The U.S. Bureau of Labor Statistics reports that median annual earnings for all workers in packaging machinery were $46,976 in 2000. Packaging machine operators and tenders earned an annual median of $19,660, with salaries ranging from $13,250 to $33,810.

Benefits vary and depend on company policy but generally include paid holidays, vacations, sick days, and medical and dental insurance. Some companies also offer tuition assistance programs, pension plans, profit sharing, and 401-K plans.

Work Environment

Packaging machinery technicians work in a variety of environments. They may work for a machinery manufacturer or in the manufacturing department of a plant or factory. Most plants are clean and well ventilated, although actual conditions vary based on the type of product manufactured and packaged. Certain types of industries and manufacturing methods can pose special problems. For example, plants involved in paperboard and paper manufacturing may have dust created from paper fibers. Workers in food plants may be exposed to strong smells from the food being processed, although most workers usually get accustomed to this. Pharmaceutical and electronic component manufacturers may require special conditions to ensure that the manufacturing environments are free from dirt, contamination, and static. Clean-air environments may be special rooms that are temperature- and moisture-controlled, and technicians may be required to wear special clothing or equipment when working in these rooms.

In general, most plants have no unusual hazards, although safety practices need to be followed when working on machinery and using tools. The work is generally not strenuous, although it does involve carrying small components and hand tools and some bending and stretching.

Most workers work 40 hours a week, although overtime may be required, especially during the installation of new machinery or when equipment malfunctions. Some technicians may be called in during the evening or on weekends to repair machinery that has shut down production operations. Installation and testing periods for new equipment can also be very time-intensive and stressful when problems develop. Troubleshooting, diagnosing problems, and repairing equipment may involve considerable time as well as trial-and-error testing until the correct solution is determined.

Technicians who work for machinery manufacturers may be required to travel to customers' plants to install new machinery or to service or maintain existing equipment. This may require overnight stays or travel to foreign locations.

Outlook

Packaging machinery technicians are in high demand both by companies that manufacture packaging machinery and by companies that use packaging machinery. With the growth of the packaging industry, which grosses more than $100 billion a year, a nationwide shortage of trained packaging technicians has developed over the last 20 years. There are far more openings than there are qualified applicants.

The packaging machinery industry is expected to continue its growth in the 21st century. American-made packaging machinery has earned a worldwide reputation for high quality and is known for its outstanding control systems and electronics. Continued success in global competition will remain important to the packaging machinery industry's prosperity and employment outlook.

The introduction of computers, robotics, fiber optics, and vision systems into the industry has added new skill requirements and job opportunities for packaging machinery technicians. There is already widespread application of computer-aided design and computer-aided manufacturing (CAD/CAM). The use of computers in packaging machinery will continue to increase, with computers communicating with other computers on the status of operations and providing diagnostic maintenance information and production statistics. The role of robotics, fiber optics, and electronics will also continue to expand. To be prepared for the jobs of the future, packaging machinery students should seek training in the newest technologies.

With packaging one of the largest industries in the United States, jobs can be found across the country, in small towns and large cities, in small companies or multiplant international corporations. The jobs are not restricted to any one industry or geographical location—wherever there is industry, there is some kind of packaging going on.

For More Information

For information on educational programs, certification, and the packaging industry, contact the following organizations:
INSTITUTE OF PACKAGING PROFESSIONALS
1601 North Bond Street, Suite 101
Naperville, IL 60563
Web: http://www.iopp.org

NATIONAL INSTITUTE FOR CERTIFICATION IN ENGINEERING TECHNOLOGIES
1420 King Street
Alexandria, VA 22314-2794
Web: http://www.nicet.org

NATIONAL INSTITUTE OF PACKAGING, HANDLING, AND LOGISTIC ENGINEERS
6902 Lyle Street
Lanham, MD 20706-3454
Web: http://users.erols.com/niphle

PACKAGING EDUCATION FORUM
4350 North Fairfax Drive, Suite 600
Arlington, VA 22203
Web: http://www.packagingeducation.org

PACKAGING MACHINERY MANUFACTURERS INSTITUTE
4350 North Fairfax Drive, Suite 600
Arlington, VA 22203
Web: http://www.pmmi.org

Index